Cambridge Elements ≡

Elements in the Philosophy of Martin Heidegger
edited by
Filippo Casati
Lehigh University
Daniel O. Dahlstrom
Boston University

HEIDEGGER ON EASTERN/ ASIAN THOUGHT

Lin Ma
Renmin University of China

CAMBRIDGE
UNIVERSITY PRESS

Shaftesbury Road, Cambridge CB2 8EA, United Kingdom

One Liberty Plaza, 20th Floor, New York, NY 10006, USA

477 Williamstown Road, Port Melbourne, VIC 3207, Australia

314–321, 3rd Floor, Plot 3, Splendor Forum, Jasola District Centre,
New Delhi – 110025, India

103 Penang Road, #05–06/07, Visioncrest Commercial, Singapore 238467

Cambridge University Press is part of Cambridge University Press & Assessment,
a department of the University of Cambridge.

We share the University's mission to contribute to society through the pursuit of
education, learning and research at the highest international levels of excellence.

www.cambridge.org
Information on this title: www.cambridge.org/9781009536738

DOI: 10.1017/9781009536721

When citing this work, please include a reference to the DOI 10.1017/9781009536721

First published 2024

A catalogue record for this publication is available from the British Library.

ISBN 978-1-009-53673-8 Hardback
ISBN 978-1-009-53669-1 Paperback
ISSN 2976-5668 (online)
ISSN 2976-565X (print)

Heidegger on Eastern/Asian Thought

Elements in the Philosophy of Martin Heidegger

DOI: 10.1017/9781009536721
First published online: May 2024

Lin Ma
Renmin University of China
Author for correspondence: Lin Ma, malin2008@ruc.edu.cn

Abstract: This Element elucidates the metamorphoses of Heidegger's comportment toward Eastern/Asian thought from the 1910s to the 1960s. With a view to the many meanings of the East at play in Heidegger's thinking, it considers how his diversified "dialogues" with the East are embedded in different phases of his *Denkweg*. Various themes unexplored previously are examined: Heidegger's early treatment of near Eastern traditions and Islamic philosophy, his views on alien cultures, the "primitive Dasein" and the "mythical Dasein," and his meditation on Russianism's deeply rooted spirituality and its recuperative possibilities for the West. Finally, this Element reveals how Heidegger opened the promise of a dialogue with the East and yet stepped back from the threshold, and how his move from the Occidental line of philosophizing toward the Oriental line is integral to his shift from the guiding question of "Being" to the abyssal question of "Beyng."

Keywords: Heidegger, Eastern thought, *Black Notebooks*, Russianism, *Zhuangzi*

ISBNs: 9781009536738 (HB), 9781009536691 (PB), 9781009536721 (OC)
ISSNs: 2976-5668 (online), 2976-565X (print)

Contents

Note on Referencing

In this Element, references to works by Heidegger and some other authors are cited by the years of their *earliest* composition or publication. This is because it is relevant to my arguments to indicate the years when (especially) Heidegger articulated a specific view. In the list of "References," these years appear in *square brackets* while the dates of later editions are set in *round brackets*.

I render *Sein* as the capitalized "Being" and *Seyn* as the capitalized "Beyng" to indicate their special status as philosophical terms. I translate *Anfang* as "inception" (instead of "beginning") and *anfänglich* as "inceptual" so as to retain the etymological connection of the words. In most cases, I refer to the German versions as published in Heidegger's *Complete Works* (*Gesamtausgabe*), which I abbreviate as GA in a reference. Since the publisher of Heidegger's *Gesamtausgabe* is always the same (that is, Vittorio Klostermann), I do not repeat this in the references. Page numbers of English translations, when available, are followed by the those of the original German editions. Whenever possible, I cite from the existing English renditions of Heidegger's works, but I have often modified the translations according to the German original. When the German version alone is available, the English translations are my own. When giving the German original for a word or a phrase in the main text, I place it in round brackets; when in a citation, I place it in square brackets.

Unless otherwise indicated, emphases in citations are all from the original texts. It is very important to keep this in mind since Heidegger frequently added emphases to his writings. Additions in round brackets and curly braces in citations are all from the original texts, and those in square brackets derive from my supplementation. For some words in the existing English translations, I adapt them to current norms. For instance, I change "man" or "men" to either "the human being" or "the humans." When the original German word is *der Mensch* I render it as "humanity."

Introduction

It is indisputable that Heidegger's thinking involves constant dialogues with Eastern/Asian thought. Far from being thoroughgoing and unitary, these dialogues assume various forms at different junctures of his path of thought – as resistance, as confrontation, as conversation, and as "deep encounter."[1] With the publication of Heidegger's *Gesamtausgabe* (*Complete Works*) almost completed, it is long overdue to treat Heidegger's comportment toward Eastern/Asian thought as a fundamental element of his philosophical enterprise. A focused study of this element has yet to be incorporated into the field of specialized Heidegger studies.[2] It is also expected to throw fresh light on Heidegger's thinking as such, and to provide a steadfast anchor for further explorations in intercultural and comparative philosophy.

This Element elucidates the metamorphoses of Heidegger's comportment toward the East/Asia from the 1910s to the 1960s. The variations of his comportment are dependent on which "East" or "Asia" is at issue, and which stage of his thinking is involved. Such terms as "East," "Asia," and "Orient" in Heidegger's own writings have complicated senses and references, but interpreters have either taken them to be abstract labels for pure otherness or reduced them to an exclusive concern with East Asian thinking. In Patrick Unruh's concordance to Heidegger's *Gesamtausgabe*, under *Asiatische* (Asiatic) are listed a dozen terms: *alte Welt* (old world), *Asien* (Asia), *ferner Osten* (Far East), *Griechen* (Greeks), *Indien* (India), *Ionien* (Ionia), *Kleinasien* (Asia Minor), *Orient*, *Ostasien* (East Asia), *Osten* (East), *östliche Welt* (Eastern world), *Russen* (Russians), and *Zen* (Unruh 2017).[3] According to this list, we can differentiate between five kinds of Asia: West Asia, South Asia, Greek Asia, Russian Asia, and East Asia; and five kinds of East: the Near East (now often replaced by "the Middle East" in a broad sense), the Greek East, the Russian East, the Indian East, and the Far East. Hence, apart from East Asian thinking, the "East" involves ancient Near Eastern traditions that had intense interaction with Greece, and it also refers to Russian thought, which figures predominantly in Heidegger's *Black Notebooks* published in the 2010s.

A few remarks on the different emphases of previously published secondary literature dealing with Heidegger's Asian connection: The edited volume entitled *Heidegger and Asian Thought*, which contains thirteen important essays, primarily focuses on initiating comparative studies. The editor Graham Parkes claims

---

[1] For "deep encounter," compare Ma 2008, 73–75.

[2] An example is the recently published *The Cambridge Heidegger Lexicon* (Wrathall 2021). Out of its 220 entries, none touches on Heidegger's thinking concerning the East or Asia.

[3] In Unruh's concordance, these terms listed under *Asiatische* do not all receive separate entries.

that comparative philosophy is "most fruitful between unconnected philosophies" while the question of influence is "of secondary significance" (Parkes 1987, 2). By contrast, Reinhard May's *Heidegger's Hidden Sources: East Asian Influences on His Work* shows an exclusive concern with demonstrating the extent to which Heidegger has drawn on East Asian thinking via a methodology of textual juxtaposition of some of Heidegger's writings and German versions of Daoist texts (May 1996). As the translator, Parkes offered the phrase "hidden sources" (culled from Heidegger's work), and he thereby withdrew his earlier claim.[4] These two books have significantly promoted studies of Heidegger in connection with Asian thought. *Heidegger on East–West Dialogue: Anticipating the Event* presents contextualized examinations of Heidegger's own ponderings on the question of East–West dialogue, revealing their potentials and problematics (Ma 2008). Since most of Heidegger's relevant remarks were made during and after World War II and were made mainly in relation to East Asia and East Asian languages, this book does not probe into those relevant themes occurring in his early work, neither does it sufficiently explore other kinds of "East" than East Asia.

The Element builds upon and yet differs from *Heidegger on East–West Dialogue* in that it aims to obtain a holistic view of all kinds of "East" insofar as Heidegger was engaged (or disengaged) with them. Consulting seventy pieces of Heidegger's original writings, it attempts to construct an account of his shifting stance on Eastern/Asian thought with an eye to the way in which it is embedded in different phases of his *Denkweg*. Hence, the coverage of this Element is much broader. Though it does not purport to elaborate on affinities or divergences between Heidegger and Eastern/Asian thought as such, it embodies implications in that direction.

Furthermore, this Element extends the timeline of the theme to the 1910s – even as early as 1908 when Heidegger attempted to learn Russian – and it draws on Heidegger's own works that have been largely neglected in studies of his Eastern connection. Some examples are his early works like *The Phenomenology of Religious Life* (1920/21), *Introduction to Phenomenological Research* (1923/24), and *Basic Concepts of Ancient Philosophy* (1926), just to mention a few prior to *Being and Time*. Moreover, this Element broaches new topics such as "primitive Dasein," "mythical Dasein," and Russianism (*Russentum*). An inquiry into the last topic has been made possible only with the recent publication of his *Black Notebooks*.

Heidegger's invocation of the East is inseparable from the rich tradition of German Oriental studies. In a way, Edward Said paid a compliment to German scholarship when he exempted it from "a protracted, sustained *national* interest in

---

[4] Reinhard May used the Latin phrase *ex oriente lux* as the original title of his book (May 1989).

the Orient" due to the limitation of Germany's overseas colonial sphere (Said 1979, 19). Advocating a "synthetic" approach and inducing other reasons for the specificity of German Oriental studies, Suzanne L. Marchand treated "German Orientalism" as more a matter of intellectual pursuits than merely a function of politics (Marchand 2009, xx; cf. xxix, xxxiii). Although the label "Orientalism" still retains one of its original meanings as the (supposedly neutral) Western discipline of studies of Asian traditions, it has lost luster due to Said's influential criticism. That is why Marchand sometimes was inclined to use the German word *Orientalistik* or the lower-case "orientalism" so as to keep it apart from the potentially ideologically loaded "Orientalism." What have taken the place of Orientalism are such terms as "Asian studies," "Near Eastern Studies," and "Islamic Studies" – terms that involve the specific areas under study. Nowadays, a more integrated approach and a global vision is being cultivated to counteract the segregation of those area studies. This development constitutes the backdrop against which this Element attempts to delve into Heidegger's thinking on the East by bringing in multifarious Eastern traditions he has encountered so that not just one single Eastern tradition is privileged at the expense of the other traditions.

The rise of modern Oriental studies in Germany was related to several events in the late eighteenth century. In 1786, Sir William Jones announced his discovery of a genealogical connection between Greek, Latin, and Sanskrit. This discovery had immediate repercussions in Germany. In his lectures "On the Language and Philosophy of the Indians" delivered in 1808, Friedrich Schlegel included the Persian and German languages in this family of resemblance, inducing numerous concrete examples of affinity (Schlegel [1808], 430–39). The attention paid to the East gave rise to what Schlegel called the "Oriental Renaissance" that could rival the Italian Renaissance. It has promoted a rewriting of the history of antiquity in the light of the newly discovered bond with the East. Schlegel devoted a lengthy discussion about the doctrine of metempsychosis and drew the conclusion that Pythagoras' philosophy was "no Hellenistic invention, although it was soon developed and adorned with all the riches of Hellenistic genius and ingenuity" (Schlegel [1808], 476). Presuming that Pythagoras had borrowed this doctrine from either Egypt or Western Asia, Schlegel strongly recommended: "We must, then, also be prepared completely to reject the oldest and proportionately best accounts of the Pythagorean philosophy" (Schlegel [1808], 476).[5]

What lies behind the infatuation of German scholars with the Oriental, especially the Indian Oriental, is an attempt at establishing a potentially divergent cultural lineage by placing an older Indian "Aryan" heritage before Greece.

---

[5] For Heidegger's connection with Schlegel, see Moore 2019.

In this way, they hoped that Germany could be set upon a *Sonderweg* (special path) apart from the prevalent Graeco-Roman-Franco "Occidental" lineage privileging English and French traditions.[6] Believing that the Indians shared the same pedigree with the Germanic people, most German Indologists enlisted the Indian epics in a quest to define German identity as "secular, Enlightened, and rational" as opposed to dogmatic and conservative Roman Catholicism that has "destroyed the ancient epic culture of the Germans" (Adluri & Bagchee 2014, 115, 119). In addition, they treated Buddhism as an Eastern analogue of Protestantism and deprecated Brahmanism in terms resembling Martin Luther's diatribe against Catholicism. German Indology enjoys the longest history and reaps the richest harvest as compared with other areas of Oriental studies despite the polemics it has given rise to.[7] German intellectuals in general were more informed of the Indian East even if they did not necessarily find in it a kindred spirit. In view of this historical and intellectual nexus, it is less possible for Heidegger to define Indian thought as "entirely different" and "wholly other," as he did with respect to East Asian thinking (though meanwhile he was also deploying such phrases for the sake of his own philosophizing; Heidegger [1953/54], 5/85, 41/126). At the same time, it becomes easier to understand why Heidegger invoked Sanskrit words in his philosophical corpus.

A prominent example of Heidegger's invocation of Sanskrit words occurs in his *Introduction to Metaphysics* (Heidegger 1935), where he mentioned two Indo-Germanic stems for the word "to be" (*sein*): one is *es*, Sanskrit *asus*, denoting "life, the living, . . . the self-standing"; the other is *bhū*, *bheu*, which receives a more originary interpretation on the basis of "the confrontation with the inception of Greek philosophy": "an emerging" that "in turn is determined by coming to presence and appearing" (Heidegger [1935], 75/54). These references long predated his inquiries in 1960 concerning whether there were possible Sanskrit words that could match his own fundamental notions such as "Being" (*Sein*), "unconcealment" (*Unverborgenheit*), and "forgetfulness" (*Vergessenheit*) (Heidegger 2001, 254/318–19; cf. Hoch 1991, 251–53). However, it can be presumed that, in Heidegger's eyes, Sanskrit as an Indo-European language also involves a subject–object structure that is conducive to metaphysical thinking. Probably for this reason, Heidegger scarcely engaged with the Indian East except for mentioning Indian Buddhism a few times and

---

[6] For a discussion of Germany's *Sonderweg*, compare McGetchin 2015, 113.

[7] For example, German Indology is perceived as an enterprise that utilized Protestant-theological and even racist preconceptions (Adluri & Bagchee 2014).

Brahma once (see Section 6). Of course, he cited "the Indies" and "the Indians" in the context of elucidating Hölderlin's poetry.[8]

Between 1880 and 1914, a period during which Heidegger was born (in 1889) and spent his earliest years, colossal archeological discoveries were made of Persian, Assyrian, and Sumerian materials that led to unprecedented large-scale specialized studies, what Marchand called the "Second Oriental Renaissance" (Marchand 2009, 157–215). Doing away with previous assumptions concerning the East recorded either in the Old Testament or by the Greeks, the studies growing out of the "Second Oriental Renaissance" suggested a strong Near Eastern influence on early Greece. This has enhanced the tendency of "Orientalizing" the history of Western culture while resisting an enduring tradition of philhellenism (cf. Marchand 2001).

This new trend of Orientalism is evidenced in Heidegger's own texts. In a review paper of 1910, Heidegger commented that for the modern intellectuals caught in the currents of "free research and free thinking," "[t]he Golden Calf, Fama, and the Babylonian Venus stood on the altars" (Heidegger [1910], 36/4). This is Heidegger's earliest reference to the East in a critical tone. In the 1915 report on the triduum commemoration held in Messkirch (Heidegger's home-town), he lamented the situation before the outbreak of World War I where people displayed "the same 'enthusiasm'" for "Indian Buddhism" and "Sumerian sun-worship" as for the "Pauper of Assisi" (Heidegger [1915a], 52). This is Heidegger's earliest reference to Buddhism and perhaps the only reference to the Sumerian culture. It is at least thirty-one years earlier than his negative remark on Buddhism in the *Contributions to Philosophy* (1936–38).[9]

The year 1915 also witnessed Heidegger's earliest citation of a central Islamic notion in a trial lecture "The Concept of Time in the Science of History" for obtaining the certification for teaching. When claiming that "the beginning of time reckoning systems show that they always begin at a historically significant event [*historisch bedeutsamen Ereignis*]," Heidegger provided in brackets three examples of this kind of event: "the founding of the city of Rome, the birth of Christ, the Hegira" (Heidegger [1915b], 75/432). The Hegira refers to Muhammad's migration from Mecca to Medina in 622, which helped the consolidation of the first Muslim community. At that time, Heidegger was not yet using *Ereignis* as a special term.

---

[8] For an account of those rare occasions where Heidegger touched on Indian thought in the early 1960s, compare Ma 2008, 161–66. In addition, in the 1966/67 seminar on Heraclitus, Heidegger mentioned: "For the Indians [*die Inder*], sleep is the highest life" (Heidegger and Fink 1979, 132/214). The English version rendered *die Inder* as "the Hindu."

[9] "No Buddhism! The opposite" (Heidegger [1936–38], 134/170). For a discussion of the full passage, compare Ma 2008, 180.

In the age of Enlightenment, German philosophers such as Leibniz and Wolff drew on the reports by the missionaries to China concerning Confucianism to construct a natural theology and ethics. With the interest shifting to Sanskrit and Indian thought, China came to stand for Oriental stagnation. Lacking any linguistic affinity with Indo-European languages and seemingly irrelevant to researches of classical antiquity (as contrasted with Near Eastern traditions), studies in the nineteenth century devoted to the Far East lagged behind, rarely being considered a part of the Academy. This forms the backdrop against which it seems a matter of course for a European like Heidegger to apply the labels of "entirely different" and "wholly other" to East-Asian thinking on various occasions (Heidegger [1953/54], 5/85, 41/126). As Marchand rightly observed, "China and Japan would only appeal to the Germans for whom classical aesthetics, Christian orthodoxy, and traditional humanistic institutions had been fully discredited" (Marchand 2009, 368).

Before the outbreak of World War I, with the social, political, and economic crises in Germany becoming ever more intense, East Asian thinking emerged in the intellectual arena. Following the appearance of close to ten renditions of the *Daodejing* 道德經 (for instance, Plaenckner 1870, Von Strauss 1870, and Ular 1903), in 1910 Martin Buber published the first translation of the *Zhuangzi* into German entitled *Discussions and Parables of Zhuangzi* (*Reden und Gleichnisse des Tschuang-tse*) using Giles' English edition as the source (Giles 1889, Buber [1910]). Buber selected fifty-four stories from the *Zhuangzi*, gave each his own title, and attached introductions of the main characters from the stories as well as an article on Daoism by himself. According to Buber, ancestor worship as advocated by Confucianism was not suitable for Europe; instead, Daoism could initiate a new path for European scholars. In 1912, Richard Wilhelm published *Zhuangzi: The True Book of South Flowerland* (*Dschuang Dsi, Das wahre Buch vom südlichen Blütenland*) in China and in Germany at the same time (Wilhelm 1912). It was directly translated from Chinese but was not a complete edition.

With the access to Chinese classics in German translations, such writers as Herman Hesse and Alfred Döblin drew on Daoist motifs in their literary works. Recalling his travels to China and India, Hesse articulated his confidence in the salvation coming from the East:

> "[H]omecoming and fruitful renewal beckon to us from that "spirit of the East" which leads from Laozi [*Lao-tse*] 老子 to Jesus, which was born of ancient Chinese art and today still speaks in every gesture of the true Asiatic" (Hesse [1916], 69).

Alongside Oswald Spengler's most influential *Decline of the West* (first volume 1918, second volume 1922), *Travel Diary of a Philosopher* by Count Hermann Keyserling (1880–1946), recording his prewar travels in India and China, also drew attention to the presumably uncorrupted spirit of the East (Keyserling 1919).[10] In 1920, Keyserling founded the School of Wisdom in Darmstadt. Like Wilhelm's China Institute established in Frankfurt in 1924, it promoted Eastern wisdom through all kinds of activities. It was also in 1924 that Paul Dahlke opened the first Buddhist temple in Europe near Berlin. In 1930, Kitayama Junyū (a Japanese scholar) completed his dissertation dealing with Buddhist metaphysics under the supervision of Karl Jaspers (cf. Kitayama 1934).

Because East Asian traditions were normally not included in the curriculum of philosophy, they rarely received any serious attention in the circle of philosophy, let alone scholarly research. Ernst Cassirer's philosophy of culture is an exception, though Heidegger quibbled at his neo-Kantian approach.[11] In *The Way into Philosophy*, published in 1926, Georg Misch strongly commended Chinese philosophy, and he opened the second chapter of his book with Zhuangzi's 莊子 vision of the boundless world in "Autumn Floods," regarding it as a breaking-through of the natural outlook on life and thus as the beginning of philosophy (Misch 1926). Since Heidegger had contact with Misch starting from 1922, and they maintained correspondence till at least the end of 1920s, he may well have been aware of this book by Misch.[12]

East Asian thinking appealed to the young Heidegger as well. Although he has always remained silent about his reading of German renditions of Daoist texts in his early life, in the 1945 "Evening Conversation," Heidegger revealed a connection (in the role of the "Older Man").

> But in order to say good night and maybe to thank you as well, I would still like to relate to you a short conversation [*ein kurzes Gespräch*] between two thinkers, which in my student years I copied down from a historiological account of Chinese philosophy because it struck me, though I did not quite understand it earlier. This evening it first became bright around me, and therefore this conversation well occurred to me. The names of the two thinkers escape me. (Heidegger[1945], 156/239)

This interlude is of the nature of autobiography and is comparable to Heidegger's later account of his sustained inquiry into the essence of language in "A Dialogue on Language" inasmuch as invention and factuality are mixed (Heidegger [1953/54]). Since Heidegger completed his Habilitation thesis in 1915, it is likely that he read German versions of the *Zhuangzi* in the early 1910s.

---

[10] Karl Löwith mentioned Keyserling three times in his correspondence with Heidegger in 1921 (Heidegger and Löwith 2021, 22, 27, 43).

[11] I address Heidegger's criticism of Cassirer in Section 2 of this Element.

[12] In a footnote of *Being and Time*, Heidegger mentioned Misch for his contribution to Dilthey studies (Heidegger [1927], 498 note xiv/399 note 1).

Starting from 1919, Heidegger had contact with a number of Japanese scholars who studied in Freiburg, and this constituted an important channel for his knowledge of Japanese ideas and art.[13] Japanese art was transmitted to Europe much earlier. In 1862, following Japan's opening to the West in 1858, over 600 Japanese works of art and artifacts were displayed at London's International Exposition and made a sensation. What European artists found the most impressive were the vivid colors and different perspectives of Ukiyo-e woodblock prints (浮世絵). What was called *Japonisme* played a role in the birth of modern art. Japanese works of art were also collected by the citizens in Bremen, a business city that is situated in northern Germany with a harbor and is well connected with the outside world, being the earliest German city that initiated trade relations with China in 1861. During his first visit to Bremen in October 1930, where he read out the parable about the joy of fish from Buber's translation (originally from chapter 17 of the *Zhuangzi*) after having delivered the lecture "On the Essence of Truth" to a gathering of nonacademic philosophers, Heidegger viewed a collection of East Asian artworks (Buber [1910], 59).[14] According to Heinrich W. Petzet – Heidegger's lifelong friend who organized his various visits to Bremen from 1930 to 1962 – he very much appreciated the (Ukiyo-e) woodblock prints by Sharaku Toshusai and Kokusai Ozaki, and found impressive a work by Utamaro Kitagawa (Petzet 1993, 169). In 1954, to celebrate Heidegger's seventy-fifth birthday, Petzet gave him an engraving by Moronobu Hishikawa (who is regarded as the founder of the style of Ukiyo-e woodblock prints) from his family collection, which depicts a Zen monastery. Heidegger hung it in his study next to two rolls with a couplet from chapter 15 of the *Daodejing* (Petzet 1993, 169). In the same year (1954), Heidegger observed (the observation is published in GA 100 – part of his nine-volume *Black Notebooks*): "Early, before World War I, the import of products [*Erzeugnisse*] of East Asian spirit – its art and poetry – had started. Many of

---

[13] According to Imamichi Tomonobu's (1922–2012) account, before leaving Germany in 1919, Itō Kichinosuke (one of his teachers) gave Heidegger a copy of the German version of Okakura Kakuzō's *The Book of Tea* (originally published in English). The phrase "Kunst des In-der-Welt-Seins" (art of Being-in-the-world) appeared in that book in relation to Daoism (Okakura 1919, 31). Itō believed that this phrase is the direct source for Heidegger's term of Being-in-the-world (cf. Imamichi 2004, 123).

[14] This is the first time that Heidegger cited the *Zhuangzi* (cf. Petzet 1993, 17–19). There are various versions of the lecture "On the Essence of Truth." The one delivered in Bremen is included in volume 80.1 of Heidegger's *Gesamtausgabe* and is dated October 8, 1930 (Heidegger [1930]). In a footnote of the lecture "On the Essence of Truth" delivered in Bremen, Heidegger quoted a verse from chapter 28 of the *Daodejing*: "The one who knows lightness, conceals him/herself in darkness" (*Der seine Helle kennt, sich in sein Dunkel hüllt*) (Heidegger [1930], 370 note 60). He cited from von Strauss' rendition except for changing the word *Wer* into *Der* (Von Strauss [1870], 140). Although this citation was removed in other versions of "On the Essence of Truth," this is the earliest occasion of Heidegger citing from the *Daodejing*.

today's European thinkers [*Geister*] and writers survive on this import secretively"(Heidegger 2020, 109). Heidegger himself should be counted among the European thinkers who drew on East Asian art and poetry that entered the European world before World War I.[15] Nonetheless, Heidegger continued to remark on a critical note:

> However – *wherein* was it imported? – *for what* did such use/abuse [*Vernutzung*] happen? – So long as we do not find the originary inception of Western-European destiny [*abendländisch-europäischen Geschickes*] that is hinting in advance, no such region opens, a region in which could be prepared a real encounter [*Begegnung*] of the "West" [*Westens*] with the Far East [*fernen Osten*]. (Heidegger 2020, 109)

This remark discloses Heidegger's suspicion concerning the relevance of such "products" imported from East Asia. It also indicates Heidegger's insistence that the enactment of the other inception of Western destiny via a dialogue with the early Greek thinkers is the necessary condition of possibility for an East–West dialogue. As is the case on other occasions, both terms of East (*Osten*) and "West" – the German original is *Westen* rather than *Abendland* – for Heidegger indicate the planetary world under the domination of the *Ge-stell*.[16] The consequence is that neither Westerners nor Asians of the current age are able to hear what was said in the old traditions, especially Asian traditions. Since the planetary world is derived from the Greek origin and since it has distorted the Greek essence, before one can speak of the possibility of a real encounter of East and West, one should first engage in a dialogue with the early Greek thinkers who were first called by Being and who had enacted the first inception of philosophy.

For his entire life, Heidegger remained entrenched in the dilemma concerning how to provide a proper account of Eastern/Asian thought without losing the pivotal weight of the Greek inception of philosophy. In this Element, I reveal the vicissitudes of his comportment in different phases of his *Denkweg*. In Section 1, I first address Heidegger's treatment of near Eastern traditions in *The Phenomenology of Religious Life* (Heidegger [1920/21]). Taking his comments on Islam as the cue, I discuss his connection with Islamic philosophy from 1915 to 1943. Heidegger's various references exhibited a degree of familiarity with Islamic philosophy, but he mainly treated it as a mediation of Aristotelian philosophy that has lost its Greek originariness.

---

[15] For a detailed discussion of Heidegger's connection with East Asian art, compare Ma and van Brakel 2014. One source that is not covered there is Heidegger's "Notes on Klee" written in 1957–8, in which he commented that Zen and the Nothing is not the representation of beings, but "the leading of the human being to the space-granting Nothing [*Nichts*]" (Heidegger [1957/58], 11).

[16] The difference between *Westen* and *Abendland* is similar to that between *westlich* and *Abendland* on which I elaborate in Section 4.

Section 2 is devoted to relevant themes occurring in *Being and Time*. I first address Heidegger's stance on the question of Eastern influences on the formation of the Western tradition. Heidegger's dismissal of the significance of such influences is connected with his emphasis on an originary unity between the ontic and the "Historical" (*Historisch*; in the context of discussing Count Yorck von Wartenburg) and with his opposition to syncretistic methodology. Then I inquire into Heidegger's thought on the "most remote and most alien cultures" (*den entlegensten und fremdesten Kulturen*) in *Being and Time* (Heidegger [1927a], 43/21). Heidegger insisted that Dasein's self-understanding must be achieved by starting from itself, keeping away from all kinds of distractions of alien cultures. However, his remarks on "primitive Dasein" and "mythical Dasein" display ambiguities and show potential for exceeding his framework of analysis of Dasein.

In the 1930s, Heidegger turned away from approaching the question of Being via fundamental ontology to a more focused concern with the history of Beyng.[17] Such a unique history is essentially bound up with the first inception of philosophy in early Greece and the destiny of the *Abendland*. This is continuous with his early emphasis on an originary unity between the ontic and the "Historical," with the Greek inception as the only "ontic" happening that can live up to such a unity. Against this backdrop, he dismissed the philosophical significance of "primitive Dasein" and "mythical Dasein" except for that of the Greek mythical Dasein. In this context, Heidegger probed into the early Greeks' "confrontation" (*Auseinandersetzung*) with the Asiatic.[18] In Section 3, I focus on this theme and I argue that we can discern two different meanings of the Asiatic under Heidegger's pen: One is the *Greek Asiatic*, what can be called "the Being-historical Asiatic"; the other is the *alien Asiatic*, what is "the most alien and most difficult" (Heidegger [1937], 21).[19] This differentiation (unarticulated by Heidegger himself) resonates with Nietzsche's distinction between the "Dionysiac Greeks" and the "Dionysiac barbarians."

---

[17] Elucidating the difference and identity of Heidegger's use of Being/Beyng (*Sein*/*Seyn*) requires more space than allowed here. Broadly speaking, Being is related to what Heidegger saw as the metaphysical approach, and Beyng (a term that Heidegger started to use in the mid-1930s) is related to the nonmetaphysical approach.

[18] The German word *Auseinandersetzung* literally means setting out (*Setzung*) from (*aus*) one another (*einander*). Its connotations range between two opposite poles. On the one hand, it has the positive meaning of "conversation" or "dialogue." On the other hand, it has the possibly negative meaning of "struggle," "contest," or "controversy." Hence, *Auseinandersetzung* can be translated differently in various contexts of Heidegger's writings in accordance with the emphases he put on this word (cf. Ma 2008, 100–3 for more).

[19] The 1966 edition of the Webster dictionary specified that the word "Asiatic" was "now often taken to be offensive," without explaining why (Grove 1966). Probably this is because it has been involved with the history of colonialism.

Although Heidegger traced the starting point of his meditation on Russianism (*Russentum*) to 1908–9 (cf. Heidegger [1939–41], 115/148), it is in the late 1930s and the early 1940s that he committed his meditation to paper in the *Black Notebooks*. In Section 4, using Dostoevsky's views as a cue, I first delineate the complicated sense in which Russia is regarded as Asiatic. Then I investigate the emergence of Russian thinkers in Heidegger's own writings, his references to Russia in terms of Asiatic in the early and middle 1930s, and his differentiation between Bolshevism and Russianism. According to Heidegger, the doctrine of Holy Sophia – a doctrine that involved no dualism of the spiritual and the material – remained alive in Russian mysticism. For him, Russianism embodies "the fervor for meditation" (*Leidenschaft der Besinnung*) and is essentially bound up with a deeply rooted spirituality, a spirituality that would be recuperative for the West (*Abendland*) standing on the brink of complete devastation and yet this spirituality needed liberation (Heidegger [1939–41], 44/56). This consideration lies concealed in Heidegger's discussion of a confrontation between Germanism and Russianism out of the history of Beyng. However, such a confrontation should not be treated as being purely internal to the legacies of Europe. Behind it is concealed a deeper and even abyssal confrontation of the West (*Abendland*) with the Asiatic. Heidegger refrained from spelling out the signification of the Asiatic in this context; Instead, he more often used the word "East" (*Ost*) to refer to both the surface Russia – that is, Bolshevik Russia as part of machination and the planetary – and the concealed Russia/Russianism that embodied a rich mystic and spiritual tradition.

Recent scholarship has attached great importance to Heidegger's "Daoist turn," building on his citation of a short passage from chapter 26 of the *Zhuangzi* concerning "the necessity of the unneeded [*die Notwendigkeit des Unnötigen*]" in "Evening Conversation: In a Prisoner of War Camp in Russia, between a Younger and an Older Man" (Heidegger [1945], 156/239).[20] In Section 5, I present a contextualized discussion of Heidegger's appropriation of the *Zhuangzi* in the 1940s, tracing the earlier emergence of this citation in his letters written in March 1945. I expound his discussion of Beyng in terms of the un-needed (*Un-nötige*) or the ne-cessity (*Not-wendige*) in his writings of the late 1930s; I also draw attention to his identification of freedom and necessity in a text of 1943/44. I argue that Heidegger's connection with the *Zhuangzi* in the 1940s must be appreciated against the larger framework of his consideration of the promise of recuperation from the Russian East as a sort of Beyng-historical East and from East *Asia* as a sort of Beyng-historical Asia.

In the last section, I first address Hölderlin's view on the relations between the "Oriental," the Greeks, and the Germans. This serves as a foil for explicating the

---

[20] An example of this scholarship is Xia 2021.

subtle changes of Heidegger's standing on the confrontation/engagement with the Asiatic/Asia in *Sojourns*, a record of his reflections during his first journey to Greece in 1962. I demonstrate the ways in which Heidegger's invocation of this theme differed from his comportment in the 1930s, which can be called a Nietzschean oppositional model. Heidegger no longer employed the negative terms regarding the Asiatic as he used earlier and instead spoke of the confrontation/engagement as "a fruitful necessity" (Heidegger [1962b], 25/228). His comportment in the 1960s can be called a Hölderlinean nondialectical model.

We can see that Heidegger's considerations are multifaceted and vary across time. Equally important is the wide spectrum of the variegated kinds of "East" with which his thinking has been involved. The Eastern traditions and Islamic philosophy entail the Near East, what is nowadays called the Middle East. Such titles as alien cultures, "primitive Dasein," and "mythical Dasein" do not bear indications as to whether they are directly related to a kind of East and, if so, with which East they are concerned, but an investigation of Heidegger's treatment of these themes in *Being and Time* and other early work well disclose his ambivalent stance on "the other" to the Western tradition. When it comes to his invocation of the early Greeks' confrontation with the Asiatic, what is involved is the Near East, in particular Persian thought. What I call the "Beyng-historical" Asiatic is fundamentally related to the Greek East (that is, Greece insofar as it is viewed as the "East"). Heidegger's meditation on Russianism bears on the Russian East with a Mongolian-Tartarian legacy, and his appropriation of the *Zhuangzi* is an adventure into the Far East. On some occasions, he attempted to encompass all kinds of "East" under the umbrella of the first inception in the *Morgenland* and the possible other inception of philosophy in the *Abendland*. At last, in view of the contributions that various kinds of "East" have rendered and could still render, Heidegger formulated a different configuration of what was at stake with the confrontation/engagement with Asia/Asiatic in the *Sojourns*.

1 Near Eastern Traditions and Islamic Philosophy

Immersed in the *Zeitgeist* that was infused with the excitement with the light from the East (*ex oriente lux*), Heidegger was exposed to all kinds of Eastern traditions. However, he diagnosed the flourishment of Oriental studies as "the clearest symptoms of the spiritual helplessness of our time," and, as an example, he mentioned the "distant [*entfernter*] cultural circles (Indian wisdom)" (Heidegger [1925], 239/50).[21] In a letter to Karl Löwith dated September 13, 1920, Heidegger cautioned against the "'danger' of making 'relativism' into a standpoint" in connection with Spengler's *Decline of the West* (Heidegger and

---

[21] The word *entfernter* was translated as "exotic" in the English edition. I changed it to "distant."

Löwith 2021, 7). He also commented that what Spengler provided "is merely a botany disguised as history" such that "[our] own present is itself only one among other [species of the present]" (Heidegger [1925], 271). Against the "danger" of a relativistic stance, Heidegger advocated using the relevance to the question of Being as the measuring rod for evaluating distance and nearness to authenticity, but he had no intention to develop a speculative system resembling Hegel's that could encompass all the possible forms of culture or tradition. This general comportment finds best reflection in the early Heidegger's remarks on Near Eastern traditions, especially those in the 1920/21 lecture course on the phenomenology of religious life.

In that lecture course, Heidegger reviewed the prevalent trend in historical studies of religion, which abrogated the eternal validity of eschatology and delved into the origin and lineage of religions in diverse Eastern traditions. As a result, "one is led to late Judaism, further to ancient Judaism, finally to ancient Babylonian and ancient Iranian notions of the decline of the world" (Heidegger [1920/21], 78/110). Heidegger considered that this approach was "object-historical" [*objektsgeschichtlich*] and missed what was at stake with eschatology. He argued that eschatology was never primarily an idea (*Vorstellung*), but rather must be appreciated from out of the event of Paul's pronouncement, precisely the pronouncement that established the dogma of eschatology. In stressing the "original complex of enactment [*Vollzugszusammenhang*] in which the eschato-logical is found for Paul," Heidegger suggested that its importance should be evaluated "independently of connections that exist between Persian and Jewish eschatological ideas" (Heidegger [1920/21], 79/111). For him, the eschatological was so uniquely bound up with the original complex of enactment that one should not apply Husserl's methodology of eidetic phenomenology to it. As Heidegger put it: "That which Paul says has a peculiar expressive function, from which one cannot tear out the 'ideational content,' in order, for instance, to compare it with the content of ancient Babylonian ideas" (Heidegger [1920/21], 79/111).

For Heidegger, any comparative study of religion that connected Christian dogmas with other Eastern traditions amounted to treating these dogmas as abstract ideas alienated from their particular enactments. We can sense that Heidegger set a very strong emphasis on positivity. The problem is that, as Heidegger himself was aware, Christianity is not the only positive religion; how, then, to deal with the tension between multiple positive religions? In *The Phenomenology of Religious Life*, Heidegger articulated the tension between universalism and relativism.

> The philosophy of the history of religion, further, has to comprehend the present and predetermine the future development of religion. It has to decide whether a universal religion of reason will come about, one which would

syncretistically emerge out of the present world religions (a *Protestant Catholicism* according to *Söderblom*), or whether in the future one of the positive religions (Christianity, Buddhism, Islam) will reign alone.[22] (Heidegger [1920/21], 17/23)

The locution of "a universal religion of reason" implicitly refers to Kantian rationalism, which could mediate the historically significant events such that their positivity would be weakened, if not completely purged. This is because the suggestion of synthesis implies that each religion contains an "ideational content," which can be abstracted from its original enactment. Heidegger would favor an approach that pivots on the entanglement of three vectors of temporality (or historicality), namely, past, present, and future, which meanwhile retains the characteristic positivity. The mention of Buddhism and Islam testifies to the fact that religious studies around that time was rather inclusive. Heidegger certainly would not endorse the Kantian universal religion of reason that was unanchored from positive historic enactments, but he did not provide a hint at the solution of relativism, one consequence of which is the autocracy, so to speak, of a single religion, as he sensed at the end of the cited observation.

After 1921, Heidegger never again delivered a lecture course on phenomenology of religion, nor did he make any comment on Islam, and yet he had a connection with Islamic philosophy, a connection that has rarely been addressed. Heidegger's 1915 Habilitation thesis dealt with Duns Scotus, and it was Avicenna's (980–1037, whose Persian name is Ibn Sina) work that constituted the starting point of Scotus' thinking.[23] Heidegger's thesis contained two citations of Latin texts in which Avicenna appeared by name (Heidegger [1915], 222 note 16; 238 note 40). Both Thomas Aquinas and Meister Eckhart – Heidegger seriously engaged with the former and drew significant inspiration from the latter – acknowledged their intellectual debts to Avicenna and Averroes (1126–1198, whose Persian name is Ibn Rushd) (cf. Caputo 1978, 1982).[24]

In a number of writings in the 1920s and 1930s, Heidegger referred to "Arabic philosophy," especially in relation to its theory of truth.[25] In the 1923/24 lecture course "Introduction to Phenomenological Research," he commented that the "*conformitas* [of the thing and the intellect] was characterized as *adaequatio*

---

[22] Both additions in brackets and emphases are from the original.

[23] For an in-depth treatment of Heidegger's connection with Avicenna, see El-Bizri 2000. For Avicenna's Influence on Duns Scotus, for instance, concerning the proof for the existence of God, see Druart 1988.

[24] According to some scholars, Aquinas was indebted to yet another Persian philosopher, Ibn Arabi (1165–1240) (cf. Mirsepassi 2019, 239).

[25] A recent book offered an account of Heidegger's reception in the Islamicate world and included a series of comparative studies (Moser et. al., 2019), but it did not focus on Heidegger's references to Islamic philosophy in his own *oeuvre*.

[adequation] in the Jewish-Arabian philosophy of the Middle Ages or rather in their Latin translations" (Heidegger [1923/24], 128/171–72). In the lecture "On the Essence of Truth" delivered on Pentecost Monday 1926, he mentioned that medieval philosophy received the definition of truth as *adaequatio* "from Boethius and from the Arabs," and "[b]y way of the Arabs it comes to Thomas" (Heidegger [1926a], 279). In this context, Heidegger cited a tenth-century work – "Book of Definitions" – by Isaac Israeli, who was one of the earliest medieval Jewish Neoplatonist writers who wrote in Arabic. In the 1927 lecture course "The Basic Problems of Phenomenology," Heidegger stated that the question of the relationship between *essentia* and *existentia* "can be traced back to Arabic philosophy, above all to Avicenna and his commentary on Aristotle," and yet "Arabic Aristotelianism is influenced essentially by Neoplatonism and by a work that played a great role in the Middle ages, the *Liber de causis* (Book of Causes)" (Heidegger [1927b], 81/113).[26] The *Liber de causis* is a short treatise on Neoplatonist metaphysics composed in Arabic by an unknown author probably in the ninth century in Baghdad. Through its twelfth-century Latin translation, it played an important role in the development of medieval Western philosophy.

Heidegger's familiarity with contributions made by Islamic philosophers is noteworthy. In fact, instead of "Arabic philosophy," it is more appropriate to use the rubric of "Islamic philosophy." This is because Iranian philosophers such as Avicenna and Suhrawardī (1155–1191 – who was considered "the Platonist of Persia") – sometimes wrote in Persian and sometimes in Arabic while some others – for instance, the Ismaili philosophers – wrote only in Persian. Historians of Western philosophy used the label "Arabic philosophy" to refer to the episode when in the twelfth-century scholars started a large-scale translation project in Toledo in Spain and in Sicily in Italy, rendering into Latin ancient Greek philosophical texts from their Arabic-language versions (occasionally via the medium of their Syrian renditions), which were the only versions available at that time. In the meantime, Arabic-language commentaries on those Greek texts as well as monographs were also translated into Latin, which exerted significant influences on the medieval Western philosophers.

Heidegger exhibited clear awareness of this history of Islamic contribution to philosophy in the lecture course "History of Philosophy from Thomas von Aquinas to Kant," during which he commented:

> Reception of Aristotelian philosophy in the system of beliefs. Hardly a representation of these spiritual rivalries, which do not proceed without severe struggle [*Kampfe*].

---

[26] For a detailed treatment of Heidegger's connection with Avicenna, see El-Bizri 2000.

> Aristotle with the Syrians and Persians, from Arabic culture there till
> toward Spain and so in Christian culture. With the downfall of Arabic
> culture, Christianity strengthens this work. Latinized philosophy of
> Arabic Aristotelianism. (Heidegger [1926/27], 44)

In this place, Heidegger conveyed his dissatisfaction with the distortion of
Aristotelian philosophy. What he called "Arabic culture" was instrumental in
this distortion. In the 1929/1930 "Fundamental Concepts of Metaphysics,"
Heidegger also drew attention to the role of "Arabic philosophy" in the "the
assimilation of the content of Christian faith to the philosophical content of
Aristotle's writings" (Heidegger [1929/1930], 43/65).

In the 1930s and 1940s, when Heidegger turned to focus on the early Greek
thinkers as the founders of Western philosophy, he came to stress that the
Islamic presentation of Aristotelian philosophy was *"completely un-Greek"*
(Heidegger [1933/34], 48/60). Later, when reiterating the latter point, he said
that Aristotle was understood "in a medieval fashion, that is, in an Arabic-
Jewish-Christian way" rather than "from the inception of thoughtful-poetic
Greek Dasein" (Heidegger [1937/38], 185/221). In the *Contributions to
Philosophy*, Heidegger several times spoke of "Judeo-Christian" and yet left
out the "Arabic" (Heidegger [1936–38], 100/126, 165/211, 325/411). In the
1943 lecture course on Heraclitus, however, Heidegger observed:

> [That] the philosophy of Aristotle as an expression of Greek thought in its
> originary directness, remains closed to us, is owed to the fact that the
> philosophy of Aristotle, by way of Jewish–Arab thought in the Middle
> Ages, was transformed by ecclesiastical theology into an entity that has
> only the words in common with the Greek Aristotle, and even these are
> translated into the language of Latin. (Heidegger [1943a], 57/74)

This is perhaps Heidegger's last reference to "Arabic" philosophy in his
major work.[27] Clearly, he referred to it insofar as it was considered as a part
of medieval (Occidental) philosophy that has lost the originariness of the
Greekness of Aristotelian philosophy and instead promoted an ontotheology
that he was determined to destroy. In doing this, Heidegger has completely
neglected the Eastern (especially Persian) constituents of Islamic philosophy,
with al-Suhrawardî as a prominent representative. As a result, Islamic philosophy was reduced to a short-lived episode in the standard history of (Western)
philosophy, which lasted from the ninth to the twelfth century. However,
contrary to what historians of Western philosophy told us, philosophy in the

---

[27] In an undated note from GA 73.1 (probably from the 1940s), Heidegger mentioned Avicenna in
relation to the notion of "actus esssendi" and commented that the word "actus" was no longer
Greek; he added that the proposition of Jewish-Arabic Aristotelianism and Scholasticism was
not "philosophically grounded and experienced" (Heidegger 2013, 155).

Islamicate world did not perish with the death of Averroes in 1198. As Henry Corbin – an acclaimed scholar of Persian tradition – observed:

> [A]t the same time in the East, and particularly in Iran, the work of al-Suhrawardī was opening up the road which so many thinkers and spiritual seekers were to follow down to our own days. (Corbin 1993, 205)

Moreover, Islamic philosophers do not consider themselves as merely spokespersons of the Greek tradition. According to Al-Farabi (c. 870–c. 950), the birthplace of philosophy was in Iraq. From there it was transmitted to Egypt and then to Greece. Later, the philosophical texts were rendered back into Syriac and Arabic. Al-Farabi envisioned the rebirth of philosophy in Iraq, its original homeland (cf. Kraemer 2003, 39). From 1930 to 1941, Heidegger had contact and face-to-face conversations with Corbin, who prepared the first French translation of a collection of Heidegger's works (Heidegger 1938). The earliest time when Corbin met Heidegger was on April 24, 1931. On various encounters, he could have informed Heidegger of the Eastern portion of Islamic philosophy. While still a student, Corbin wrote down numerous Arabic or Persian glosses and sometimes provided counterparts to Heidegger's terms in the margins of his own copy of *Being and Time*, for instance, مفهوم for *Begriff* (concept), معنی for *Sinn* (sense), and اِنفَ عَ. for *Affektion* (affection) (Camilleri and Proulx 2014, 48, 55).[28] It remains unknown whether Corbin discussed these terms with Heidegger. Nonetheless, as a philosopher of great curiosity, Heidegger could have put forward inquiries about Persian thought. At least, Corbin's presence could have reminded Heidegger of Greeks' earliest encounter with Persia, with the Greco-Persian wars in the fifth century BCE as a climax.

2 Alien Cultures, Primitive Dasein, and Mythical Dasein

Being and Time does not contain a reference to any specific Eastern tradition, but we can discern a shadow of the East between the lines, for instance, in such phrases as the "most remote and most alien cultures," "primitive Dasein," and "mythical Dasein" (see the citations in this section). In the Introduction to *Being and Time*, Heidegger deplores the situation that Dasein

> confines its interest to the multiformity of possible types, directions, and standpoints of philosophical activity in the most remote and most alien [*entlegensten und fremdesten*] cultures; and by this very interest it seeks to veil its own groundlessness. Consequently, despite all its historiological interests and all its zeal for a philologically 'objective' [*sachliche*] Interpretation, Dasein no longer understands the most elementary conditions

---

[28] This document contains some correspondence between Heidegger and Corbin.

which would alone make a positive return [*Rückgang*] to the past [*Vergangenheit*] possible – in the sense of a productive appropriation [*Aneignung*]. (Heidegger [1927a], 43/21)[29]

These negative remarks on "the most remote and most alien cultures" resonate with Heidegger's earlier disparagement in 1915 of the wide-spread zeal for Buddhism and Sumerian sun-worship. The expression "philologically 'object-ive'" recalls the fervor of the German scholars for miscellaneous Eastern languages. According to Heidegger, such a fervor precisely disguised Dasein's own lack of ground, which could only be recuperated by productively appropriating its own *past* – an important dimension of true historicality. Heidegger distinguished between objective historiology (*Historie*) that aimed at recording and reporting the events in the presumably linear course of time, on which basis equal attention was paid to the events from remote and alien cultures, and historicality (*Geschichtlichkeit*) that was tied to Dasein and enables it to study history.

In a later section from Division Two of *Being and Time*, Heidegger again emphasized that "the very prevalence of a differentiated interest even in the most remote and most primitive cultures is in itself no proof of the authentic historicality of a 'time'" (Heidegger [1927a], 448/396). Against the tide hailing the import of a wide range of alien cultures, Heidegger urged for the rehabilita-tion of the authentic historicality.

One way to "make a positive return to the past" is an overall reinterpretation – or destruction (*Destruktion*), to use Heidegger's own word – of the Western philosophical tradition. In doing this, Heidegger admonishes that one should shield against records about nonessential Eastern influences on the formation of Western tradition. He cites at length from Yorck's letter to Wilhelm Dilthey (in section 77 from Division Two of *Being and Time*):

> We must keep wholly aloof from all such rubbish, for instance, as how often Plato was in Magna Graecia or Syracuse. On this nothing vital depends. This external fashion [*äußerliche Manier*] which I have seen through critically, winds up at last with a big question-mark and is put to shame by the great Realities of Homer, Plato, and the New Testament. (cited in Heidegger [1927a], 452/400)

---

[29] The word *entlegensten* has been translated as "exotic" in the received English versions. Although I provide references to J. Macquarrie and E. Robinson's version of *Being and Time*, in most cases I have also consulted J. Stambaugh's rendition (New York: State University of New York Press, 1996). The German word *Interpretation* (translated as the capitalized "Interpretation") mainly denotes systematic philological exegesis and should be distinguished from Heidegger's favored notion of *Auslegung* (translated as the lower-case "interpretation"), which applies to any interpretation of a particular entity as something.

Magna Graecia or Syracuse was located in Southern Italy. A more common story was that Plato, as well as other Greek philosophers such as Thales and Pythagoras, studied in Egypt for quite some years (cf. West 1971, 3). As is recognized among specialists, the early Greek thinkers themselves, including Aristotle, did not advocate a Greek origin of philosophy. Rather, they traced the origins of philosophy to earlier non-Greek peoples (cf. Momigliano 1975, Laks 2018). The sophist Hippias of Elis (fl. fifth century BCE) provided a list of similarities between the ideas of Greek thinkers and those of "barbarians" (cf. Laks 2018, 52). Although his main intention was to dismiss the significance of the philosophical ideas of the "foreigners," in the opening of the famous *Lives of Eminent Philosophers*, Diogenes Laertius (fl. third century) articulated a common saying around his time: "The practice of philosophy some say originated among foreigners" (Laertius 2021, 35).[30] Examples concerning these barbarian origins of philosophy are legion.

> The Persians, they say, had Magi; the Babylonians or Assyrians had Chaldeans; the Indians had Naked Sages; ... There was also Ochus in Phoenicia, Zalmoxis in Thrace, and Atlas in Libya. (Laertius 2021, 35).

Laertius presented a panoramic vision in which abundant Eastern intellectual traditions were recognized despite their later dismissal. Moreover, the wisdom of such figures as Ochus, Zalmoxis, and Atlas were included as part of the Greek legacy while as regards their background they came from the Eastern sphere. Laertius also mentioned that with the origin of philosophy with the Greeks, its name "has resisted foreign appellation" (Laertius 2021, 36, note 6). This means that there did exist foreign designations of philosophy, probably before its origin with the Greeks.

Heidegger agreed with Yorck's judgment that such alleged Eastern influences were external, dubious, and shallow. He claimed that Yorck's insight was gained "from his knowledge of the character of the Being of the human Dasein itself, not from the object of historical observation in keeping with an approach from a theory of science" (Heidegger [1927a], 453/401). The critical tone of "the object of historical observation" reminds us of his earlier dismissal of a similar "object-historical" methodology applied to eschatology, a methodology that set this kernel dogma of Christianity on the same plane of study together with Eastern traditions.

Yorck's remark resonated with Heidegger's invocation of Kant's distinction between "Plato the academic" and "Plato the letter-writer" toward the very end

---

[30] It is notable that the latest edition of Laertius' record has changed the former translation of βαρβάρων as "barbarians" into "foreigners." For example, the Loeb Classical Library edition renders the same sentence as "There are some who say that the study of philosophy had its beginning among the barbarians" (Laertius 1972, 3).

of his *Basic Problems of Phenomenology*. "Plato the academic" is the father of philosophy while "Plato the letter-writer" is an "enthusiast" (Heidegger [1927b], 328/467). Heidegger cited in full Kant's quote from Plato's seventh epistle. This epistle provided a record of Plato's activities in Syracuse and Southern Italy, and it also proffered a quasi-mystical theory of the forms, one that has inspired all kinds of mystical and figurative expressions as found in what was called philosophy of feeling (*Gefühlsphilosophie*) in Kant's time. It purported to investigate the formation of worldviews, magic, and myth. Those mystical and figurative expressions constituted an important part of the spiritual life that according to Heidegger "more than ever before threatens philosophy" of his own time and needed to be confronted (Heidegger [1927b], 328/467). The distinction between "Plato the academic" and "Plato the letter-writer" parallels Yorck's insulation of the greatness of Homer, Plato, and the New Testament from the allegedly superficial anecdotes about Plato.

Heidegger regarded Yorck as the first philosopher who, together with Wilhelm Dilthey, initiated *historicality* (*Geschichtlichkeit*) as a defining characteristic of the ontology of human beings (cf. Farin 2016), but Yorck sometimes also used the word "Historical" (*Historisch*) to convey a similar idea. In the context of discussing Yorck, Heidegger adopted Yorck's term of "Historical" (*Historisch*), which shares the same meaning as *Geschichtlichkeit*. It is tied to Dasein and resists a scientific-objective approach, which Heidegger called "historiology" (*Historie*). The "Historical" should not be identified with "historiology."[31] As Heidegger pointed out, Yorck's major criticism of Dilthey was that Dilthey failed to pay sufficient attention to the generic differentiation between the ontical and the "Historical" (Heidegger [1927a], 451/399). For Yorck, the ontic is what is there without inner life, temporality, or history; and the Historical resides in a constant play of forces and effective connections (cf. Farin 2016). Building on Yorck's idea, Heidegger advocated that, in order to conceive the Historical "categorially" in distinction from the ontical, one should first bring the ontical and the Historical into a "more originary unity" before one starts to compare them and distinguish them from each other. He added: "The idea of Being encompasses both the 'ontical' and the 'Historical.' *This* [idea] must let itself be 'generically differentiated'" (Heidegger [1927a], 455/403).

Although at this moment Heidegger did not spell out all of his concerns about an originary unity between the ontic and the Historical, the enormous output of his later work on the reinterpretation of Western philosophy stems from this presupposition. What is peculiar about this presupposition is that he had almost

---

[31] In the Index of *Being and Time*, the term "Historical" is listed separately with reference to Yorck (Heidegger [1927], 541). The German edition provides no index.

exclusively restricted such a unity to the important events of early Greece that according to him constituted the abyssal foundation of Western philosophy. That Being encompasses both the ontical and the Historical is the quintessential of the later notion of the history of Beyng as a sending that calls for a futuristic renewal.

In *Being and Time*, Heidegger downgraded the methodology of synthesis as often seen in studies of Eastern cultures. For him, the "wealth of knowledge of the most manifold and most remote cultures and forms of Dasein" seemed to be felicitous to achieve a natural conception of the world, but this was only an illusion because the real problem remained unrecognized (Heidegger [1927a], 76/52).

> The syncretistic comparison and classification of everything does not of itself offer genuine essential knowledge. Subjecting the manifold to tabulation does not guarantee a real understanding of what has been ordered. (Heidegger [1927a], 76/52)

The word "syncretistic" echoes Heidegger's earlier reference to "a universal religion of reason" that could result from a synthesis of world religions, a universal religion which Heidegger opposed. According to him, because being-in-the-world is the basic mode of Dasein's existence, one must first have a grasp of Dasein's own basic constitution so as to be in a position to appraise various pictures of the world and put them into order. In another place, Heidegger again resisted the methodology of synthesis.

> [T]he opinion may now arise that understanding the most alien cultures and "synthesizing" them with one's own may lead to Dasein's first complete and genuine enlightenment about itself. Versatile curiosity and restless "knowing-all" masquerade as a universal understanding of Dasein. (Heidegger [1927a], 222/178)

Here, we can detect a similar reason for Heidegger's disparagement of the methodology of synthesis when he countered the assumption that an "ideational content" could be isolated from Paul's message and then be drawn into comparison with ancient Babylonian ideas. What masqueraded as universalism was in fact a pseudo-universalism. It would damage the priority of Dasein's ownmost self-understanding and only amounted to curiosity lacking depth. Heidegger followed up this criticism by claiming that "[w]hen Dasein, tranquillized, and 'understand-ing' everything, thus compares itself with everything, it drifts along towards an alienation [*Entfremdung*] in which its ownmost potentiality-for-Being is hidden from it," and this alienation "*closes off* from Dasein its authenticity and possibil-ity"; however, "understanding itself is a potentiality-for-Being which must be made free in one's *ownmost* Dasein alone" (Heidegger [1927a], 222/178).

In the last analysis, Dasein's self-understanding must be achieved by starting from itself, keeping away from all kinds of distractions coming from the most manifold and most remote cultures. Hence, resistance constitutes Heidegger's general comportment toward alien cultures in *Being and Time*. However, in his remarks on "primitive Dasein," Heidegger exhibited considerable ambiguities concerning the relation between (Western) ontology as pursued under the heading of the question of Being (which in *Being and Time* was probed via analysis of Dasein because Dasein is the only entity that could raise the question of Being; hence the qualification of "fundamental" ontology) and ethnological studies of alien cultures.[32] These ambiguities can be found in section 11 of *Being and Time*. In section 10, just before broaching the topic of ethnology, Heidegger addressed the relation between fundamental ontology and anthropology, psychology, and biology. His view is that neither of these disciplines furnished an adequate analysis of the Being of Dasein. Instead, their studies were founded in one way or another upon an implicit ontology of Dasein. We will see that, although Heidegger also made similar comments about ethnology, his reflection on ethnology exceeded the framework he set up in section 10 of *Being and Time* concerning the relation between analysis of Dasein and other disciplines.[33]

Heidegger first confirmed that a focus on primitive Dasein could render positive results for analysis of Dasein and could illuminate the "ontological structures of phenomena in a genuine way" because primitive Dasein enjoys a "primordial absorption" (*ursprünglichen Aufgehen*) in the things in a way that is less concealed and less complicated (Heidegger [1927a], 76/51). In a later section, Heidegger suggested a concrete example for such a "transcultural" study: the views of death among the primitives (*den Primitiven*) and their ways of comporting themselves toward it in magic and cult throw light on the understanding of Dasein (Heidegger [1927a], 291–92/247).

This rings a positive note as regards the knowledge about "primitive peoples" provided by ethnology. Nonetheless, Heidegger claimed that, like other positive sciences, ethnology presupposes an inadequate analytic of Dasein in carrying out such work as collecting materials, sorting them out, and elaborating on

---

[32] In the lecture course for the war emergency semester of 1919, Heidegger devised what could be called a thought experiment: Should a Senegalese be transplanted into the classroom, how would he make sense of the lectern that he had never seen before? Heidegger's answer is that at least the Senegalese would see *something*. The lectern would have a meaning (*Bedeutung*) for him. His conclusion is: "The meaningful character of 'instrumental strangeness' [*zeuglichen Fremdseins*], and the meaningful character of the 'lectern', are in their essential core [*Wesenskern*] absolutely identical" (Heidegger [1919], 61/72). It seems that at that time Heidegger believed that his phenomenological analysis of experiential structure is "universally" valid – in a way – though the content of the experience could be culturally variable.

[33] In *Logic: The Question of Truth*, Heidegger remarked that psychology "has an entirely chaotic form," and that it "is being encroached [*eindrängen*] by ethnology and research into the historical possibilities of the life of the primitives" (Heidegger [1925/26], 30/36). This also shows that he recognized a difference between ethnology and psychology (at least) and that he acknowledged the challenge brought by ethnology.

them. Similarly, in the example of death, he supplemented his invocation of the primitives with the proviso that "the Interpretation [*Interpretation*, as distinguished from *Auslegung*] of this understanding already requires an existential analytic and a corresponding conception of death" (Heidegger [1927a], 292/247). However, the following remark from section 11 is highly ambivalent:

> [S]ince the positive sciences neither "can" nor should wait for the ontological labours of philosophy to be done, the further course of research will not be accomplished as "progress", but rather as repetition [*Wiederholung*] and ontologically more transparent purification of what has been ontically discovered. (Heidegger [1927a], 76/51)

In this place, Heidegger added a lengthy note referring to Cassirer's *Philosophy of Symbolic Forms. Part Two: Mythical Thought* published in 1925. While noting that Cassirer has made "mythical Dasein [*das mythische Dasein*] a theme for philosophical Interpretation [*Interpretation*]" and provided important clues for ethnological research, Heidegger was concerned whether Cassirer's Kantian methodology had laid a solid ground for those analyses and whether "a new and more primordial start [*ursprünglicheren Ansatzes*]" may be needed ((Heidegger [1927a], 490note xi/51note 1). In his review article of 1928, Heidegger more explicitly faulted Cassirer for having ignored the task of first making transparent the "ontological constitution" [*ontologischen Verfassung*] of mythical Dasein (Heidegger [1928a], 188/267). He seemed to assume that an adequate analytic of Dasein must be perfectly furnished before one sets one's feet upon the road of ethnological research.

In comparison, Heidegger's remark in *Being and Time* (cited earlier) is more profoundly ambiguous. He did not take it for granted that "the ontological labours of philosophy" are readymade to be applied to ethnology, and yet he refrained from affirming that research of the life of primitive peoples could contribute to formulating a more adequate analytic of Dasein. Nevertheless, such locutions as "repetition" and "ontologically more transparent purification" – despite the problematic of the latter phrase – strongly suggest that Heidegger expected a more intertwined interaction between ethnology (the ontical) and analysis of Dasein (the ontological). That is why it is not easy to pin down a definite referent for "the further course of research," which builds upon the interaction between these two.

In a later section in *Being and Time*, Heidegger revisited the theme of the mythical, insisting on his basic tenet that Dasein always understands itself in its very existence even if such an understanding is extremely mythical or magical.

> For otherwise, Dasein would never 'live' in a myth and would not be concerned with magic in ritual and cult. The idea of existence which we have posited gives us a sketch [*Vorzeichnung*] of the formal structure of the

understanding of Dasein and does so in a way which is not binding [*unver-bindliche*] as regards the existentiell. (Heidegger [1927a], 361/313)

As always, Heidegger wanted to maintain the priority of the existential-ontological structure of Dasein, which according to him makes possible its self-understanding in whatever way, including the mythical way. However, here the formulation "not binding" suggests that the sketch of the formal structure of the understanding of Dasein could be provisionary and revisable in the light of the "existentiell" or the ontical. This ambiguity reveals itself when Heidegger was addressing the "ontical priority of the question of Being" (section title of §4) in the Introduction to *Being and Time*. "The question of existence is one of Dasein's ontical 'affairs'. This does not require that the ontological structure of existence should be theoretically transparent" (Heidegger [1927a], 33/12). On the following page, he adds: "But the roots of the existential analytic, on its part, are ultimately existentiell, that is, ontical" (Heidegger [1927a], 34/13). Heidegger was aware that existence can never be perfectly attuned with a certain transparent ontological structure. Despite his repeated emphasis on the priority of existential analytic of Dasein, he acknowledged that the ultimate source of such an analysis is ontical, which is varied and keeps the analytic of Dasein open to revisions according to the variations of the ontical/existentiell.

Another example also displays Heidegger's vacillation between the existential and the existentiell. Heidegger agreed that citing "the abundant use of 'signs' [*Zeichen*] with primitive Dasein, as in fetishism and magic" would be helpful for illustrating the distinctive role those signs play in everyday concern (*Besorgen*) because it was presumed that in a primitive world a sign coincided with that which was indicated (Heidegger [1927a], 112/81). He pointed out, nonetheless, that the construction of signs had nothing to do with any theoretical aim or speculation; hence, interpreting fetishism and magic in accordance with a general theory of signs was insufficient for grasping "the kind of 'being-ready-to-hand' [*Zuhandenseins*] of the entities encountered in the primitive world" (Heidegger [1927a], 113/81–82). This testifies to the fact that Heidegger was on the point of ascribing a more important role to the ontical, whose significance is highlighted in the primitive world that does not embrace a general (Western) theory of signs.

Generally speaking, in Division Two of *Being and Time* (entitled "Dasein and Temporality"), Heidegger assumed a rather resolute attitude of dismissal of the significance of Eastern influences for the sake of reinvigorating Dasein's true historicality. In Division One (entitled "Preparatory Fundamental Analysis of Dasein"), while demonstrating an overarching resistance, Heidegger appeared to be more open to the possibility that Dasein's existential-ontological structure is not fixed invariably but could be modified (if not completely overhauled) on the basis of the alternative existentiell input rendered from analyses of primitive Dasein or of mythical Dasein.

In the lecture course "Introduction to Philosophy" of 1928/29, Heidegger distinguished between the Greeks as an early people and as the primitive people. He asserted, "It would be completely wrong to equate the heroic time of the Greeks with today's Kaffirs" (Heidegger [1928/29], 123). The precise designation of "Kaffirs" (nowadays regarded as an offensive term) is varied. What Heidegger had in mind might be a certain group of black Africans who were said to have no history. He emphasized that in principle the Greek Dasein must be understood according to the fundamental-ontological interpretation of Dasein instead of anthropology. On the other hand, he tried to protect mythical Dasein from being demoted to the status of a deficient mode of Being-in-the-world.

> Mythical Dasein has and knows nothing of the likes of science. This is not because the humans of this Dasein were too clumsy or even too stupid for this, but because for such a Dasein science in its very essence makes no sense at all. It is therefore one of the largest methodological blunders that permeate the earlier interpretation [*Interpretation*] of mythical Dasein until now – as in the case of the French school of sociology and ethnology– such that one explains mythical thinking in whatever sense as a preform of European-modern scientific thinking. . . . But Cassirer also fell prey to this fundamental blunder. (Heidegger [1928/29], 370)[34]

It seems that Heidegger wished to recuperate the significance of mythical Dasein as a way of being of "simplicity and 'care-lessness' [*Sorg-losigkeit*]" (cf. Heidegger [1928b], 138/174), a Being-historical significance that is more profound than the supposedly superficial accounts offered by the French socio-logical and ethnological school. However, it would turn out in my discussion in the next section that what he would like to draw on as mythical Dasein was confined to the early Greeks. One can discern a sign of this turning to the Greeks as the presumably authentic mythical Dasein in the following remark: "Cassirer has used extensive material of ethnology, but he used too much in this area, and altogether did not consult the great and richer mythology [*Mythologie*] of the Greeks" (Heidegger [1928/29], 358). No matter how unsuccessful Cassirer's Kantian methodology was, he made extensive studies of images of time as found with the Persians, the Indians, the Chinese, and the Egyptians. This

---

[34] In the lecture course "Phenomenology and Transcendental Philosophy of Value" for the summer semester of 1919, Heidegger named two French sociologists Turgot and Comte:

> Turgot discovered the law of the three stages in the development of mankind: the theological-mythical [*der theologisch-mythischen*], the metaphysical, and the positive. (This was the law that Comte later made the basis of his philosophy of history) (Heidegger [1919], 113/132–33).

presented a stark contrast with Heidegger who did not seriously consider the significance of "alien" cultures at this stage of his career. This is because for him they fell out of the essential History with which alone he was concerned, though in his review of Cassirer's book he felt obliged to mention those parts related to the Persians, the Indians, the Chinese, and the Egyptians (Heidegger [1928a], 183/259).

3 The Early Greeks and the Duplicity of the Asiatic

Another aspect of Heidegger's concern with Asian thought is his ponderings on the early Greeks' encounter with "the Asiatic" (*das Asiatische*). This theme first appeared in the mid-1920s and lasted until the late 1960s. Heidegger's relevant speeches in this connection manifest different comportments, and most of them are pervaded with profound ambiguities and resist neat characterizations. What makes Heidegger's thinking more perplexing is his idea as articulated in the early 1930s bearing on a sort of ontological power of destruction and ruination that meanwhile offers generation and preservation. He claimed that those powers were to be understood in the Greek sense, and he also called them "the Asiatic" (*das Asiatische*). Could we assimilate the significance of this "Asiatic" to the one which Heidegger presented as "the most alien and the most difficult" in speaking of the early Greeks' confrontation with the Asiatic in the middle to late 1930s? How are we to evaluate these two kinds of "Asiatic"? In this section I address these interrelated questions in the light of Nietzsche's influence on Heidegger.

In ancient times, there exist no strict borders between the regions surrounding the Mediterranean Sea, the regions that were later divided and designated as parts of three disparate continents: Europe, Asia, and Africa. Due to the facility of travelling across the sea, there were intense interaction and communication among the peoples living there. It is generally accepted that Greek sciences (in particular, mathematics and medicine) flourished out of learning from Egyptian and Babylonian sciences. Heidegger did not refrain from mentioning such a connection. In the lecture course for the war emergency semester of 1919, he remarked:

> In the essentially practically directed cultural age of Hellenism, out of the abundance of its life-possibilities flowing together from all lands [*allen Ländern*], often more [contributing] to the self-esteem of science, all science, either as knowledge or as philosophy, enters into the service of immediate life and becomes the art of its correct regulation. (Heidegger [1919], 15/18)

As Heidegger himself pointed out, in ancient times there was no strict distinction between science and philosophy, and the flourishment of Greek culture owed a debt to the variegated sources from different lands. If this particular observation remained too general, in the lecture course on Plato's

Sophist delivered in 1924, Heidegger made specific references to non-Greek culture by twice mentioning mathematics/geometry and astronomy in Egypt. On the first occasion, he said that "the first sciences" "originated in Egypt" (Heidegger [1924], 94/65). On the second occasion, he referred to Plato's use of the legend about Theuth – the Egyptian god who invented number, board games, dice, geometry, astronomy, and writing – in order to clarify "the ontological function of the free-floating *logos* in Dasein" (Heidegger [1924], 340/235–36). In the lecture course on ancient philosophy delivered in 1926, Heidegger observed:

> The Greeks and mathematics: no sources documenting the time and mode of the transmission from the Egyptians or Phoenicians through papyri. Yet the Greeks' ramified {?} commercial relations, as well as their colonies, throughout the Mediterranean area, and their voyages for purposes of trade, culture, and research all testify clearly enough that an exchange had taken place. (Heidegger [1926b], 32/40)[35]

Heidegger drew attention to the fact that the geographical location of Greece offered convenience for commercial, cultural, and scientific exchanges with other peoples such as the Egyptians and the Phoenicians. Preceding the publication of *Being and Time*, Heidegger showed clear awareness of the overlapping territories and intertwined histories in this early time of cultural flourishment. However, in the 1930s, he began to stress the uniqueness and creativeness of the Greek people and demonstrated a keen desire to insulate them from other "Asiatic" peoples. In my view, Nietzsche's distinction between the "Dionysiac Greeks" and the "Dionysiac barbarians" played an important role in this significant shift.

The shadow of a struggle with the Asiatic was present in Nietzsche's early work. This comes forth in relation to his famous contrast between the Dionysian and the Apollonian. Nietzsche mentioned Dionysus as someone who "came storming in from *Asia* [*die den aus Asien heranstürmenden Dionysos*]" (Nietzsche [1870], 121/583; emphasis added). In saying this, he acknowledged the origin of this god in Asia. He also said that the Dionysian was originally related to "a cult of nature, which, amongst *the Asians* [*bei den Asiaten*], had meant the crudest unleashing of the lower drives" (Nietzsche [1870], 121/583; emphasis added). Nietzsche described the entrance of the Dionysian as an invasion: "Never was the struggle between truth and beauty greater than when the worship of Dionysus invaded Greece" (Nietzsche [1870], 126/562). The phrases "came storming in" and "invaded" are both rather strong, signaling the tension and even conflict between "Asia" and

---

[35] The question mark after the word "ramified" is from the original.

"Greece." Moreover, with the Dionysian, nature's artistic drives attain their immediate satisfaction *"without the mediation of any human artist"* (Nietzsche [1872], 19/30). By contrast, Apollo was recognized as a Hellenic god of visual art who also taught an ethic of discreteness, moderation, and self-control.[36] Standing for clear-mindedness, order, rhythm measure, and respecting boundaries and limits, the Apollonian moderated this Dionysiac upsurge and transformed it into a festival of universal redemption. When recounting the myth that Apollo joined Dionysus after the latter had been dismembered, Nietzsche comments: "[t]his is the image of Dionysus created anew by Apollo and saved from his *Asiatic* dismemberment" (Nietzsche [1870], 124/559; emphasis added). In saying this, Nietzsche hinted at the possible emergence of a transfigured image of Hellenized Dionysus in an effort to disentangle himself from the Asiatic wildness.

Nietzsche alluded to the existence of a "vast gulf which separated the *Dionysiac Greeks* from the Dionysiac barbarians" (Nietzsche [1872], 20/31). Although the Greeks were subjected to the stirrings aroused by the Dionysiac to be Titanic and barbaric, at the same time they received admonishment as regards the principles of "Know thyself" and "Not too much" from the ethical divinity Apollo, who defused such barbaric stirrings and protected the Greeks from excessive indulgence in them (Nietzsche [1872], 27/40). By contrast, the Dionysiac festivals as held in Babylon, for instance, were characterized by unrestrained display of the wildest of nature's beasts without any mediation, redemption, or transfiguration. The Dionysiac Greeks were distinguished from the "Dionysiac barbarians" (that is to say, non-Greek Asians) in that the Greeks sought and achieved reconciliation between the opposing powers. It is only with the Greeks that "for the first time the jubilation of nature achieves expression as art" (Nietzsche, [1872], 20/32). The activities of the festival remained the same, but they were imbued with a different signification. Nonetheless, the disruptive Dionysiac force was retained and would burst out at any moment from the subterranean layer of the Apollonian consciousness.

Nietzsche was a pivot figure who effectually enhanced the ideology concerning the "Greek miracle" (a phrase formulated by the French Orientalist Ernest Renan [1823–1892]) despite the fact that, as is commonly agreed, he had a life-long interest in Indian philosophy and he professed his ideas using the Persian Zarathustra as the mouthpiece (cf. Elman 1983, Bilimoria 2008). Nietzsche played a role in encouraging the later generation of scholars to dismiss more resolutely the significance of the early Greeks' connection to the East. However,

---

[36] Some scholars pointed out that, in terms of origin, Apollo was not Hellenic but rather Asian (cf. Silk and Stern 2016, 202).

Nietzsche's own descriptions in *Philosophy in the Tragic Age of the Greeks* testified to the fact that historians in his time held a positive view concerning the early Greek encounter with the East.

> It has been pointed out assiduously, to be sure, how much the Greeks were able to find and learn abroad in the Orient, and it is doubtless true that they picked up much there. It is a strange spectacle, however, to see the alleged teachers from the Orient and their Greek disciples exhibited side by side: Zoroaster next to Heraclitus, Hindus next to Eleatics, Egyptians next to Empedocles, or even Anaxagoras amidst the Jews and Pythagoras amidst the Chinese. (Nietzsche [1873], 29/300)

Nietzsche contended that nothing significant can be discovered by such juxtapositions. For him, the quest for philosophy's "beginnings" (*Anfängen*) is trivial because what lies in all beginnings is only "crudity, formlessness, emptiness, and ugliness" (Nietzsche [1873], 30/300). What matters is "the higher levels [*höheren Stufen*]," and all the other cultures "are put to shame by the marvelously idealized philosophical company represented by the ancient Greek masters" (Nietzsche [1873], 31/301). Although the Greeks absorbed elements from other cultures, they made greater achievements by purifying, solidifying, and elevating those imported elements. For Nietzsche, the Greeks were inventors "in a higher sense and a purer sphere" because "what they invented were *the archetypes of philosophic thought*" (Nietzsche [1873], 31/301).

> Only a culture such as the Greeks possessed can answer our question as to the task of the philosopher, and only it, I repeat, can justify philosophy at all ... There is a steely necessity which binds a philosopher to a genuine culture. (Nietzsche [1873], 33/303).

In *Will to Power*, which was edited and numbered on the basis of a selection of Nietzsche's notes composed from 1883 to 1888, Nietzsche revisited his contrastive notions of the Dionysian and the Apollonian. It is here that we find a most direct connection between Heidegger and Nietzsche. In the 1929/1930 lecture course on "Fundamental Metaphysical Concepts," Heidegger deployed this pair of notions to discuss the opposition between life and spirit, and he presented the following quotation from Nietzsche as "the most profound analysis of the Greek world" (Heidegger [1929/1930], 73/110).

> This antithesis [*Gegensätzlichkeit*] of the Dionysian and the Apollinian within the Greek soul is one of the great riddles [*Räthsel*] to which I felt myself drawn when considering the nature [*Wesen*] of the Greeks. Fundamentally I was concerned with nothing except to guess why precisely Greek Apollonianism had to grow out of a Dionysian subsoil [*Untergrund*];

why the Dionysian Greek needed to become Apollinian; that is, to break his will to the terrible, multifarious, uncertain, frightful, upon a will to measure, to simplicity, to submission to rule and concept. The immoderate, disorderly Asiatic [*Das Maasslose, Wüste, Asiatische*] lies at his roots [*Grunde*]: the bravery of the Greek consists in his struggle [*Kampfe*] with his Asiaticism [*Asiatismus*]; beauty is not given to him, as little as is logic or the naturalness of customs – it is conquered, willed, won by struggle – it is his *victory* [*Sieg*]. (Nietzsche 1968, 539–540)

The English version of Heidegger's *Fundamental Metaphysical Concepts* did not follow this translation by Walter Kaufmann.[37] The word *Gegensätzlichkeit* is translated as "opposition" in the Heidegger version, but "antithesis" in the Kaufmann version sounds more conceptual, entailing a quasi-dialectical internal relation between the two. Kaufmann translated *Maasslose* and *Wüste* as two adjectives describing das *Asiatische*, but these three words are actually three independent substantives, though they stem from their adjective forms. Furthermore, "the immoderate" is better than "the immeasurable" in the Heidegger version while "the desolate" is more precise than "disorderly" in the Kaufmann version. Hence, we have "The immoderate, the desolate, the Asiatic" as an alternative rendition of *Das Maasslose, Wüste, Asiatische*.

We can see that, when in the 1880s Nietzsche revisited the antithesis of the Dionysian and the Apollonian, his attention was focused on the tension between these two terms as much as on their mutual bond, both abiding in the nature of the Greeks. Yet, the Dionysian remained attached to the Asiatic as associated with the "immoderate" and the "desolate," which lay at the "ground" of the Greeks. Moreover, the achievement by the Apollonian did not fall from the sky. Instead, beauty, logic, and morals were all acquired through struggle and conquest.

Heidegger's concern with Greek antiquity was set in a larger framework of a concern with the destiny of the "West" [*Abendland*]. He was aware that distinctions of the terms "Western" and the "West' versus the East, the Oriental, and the Asiatic initially only indicated geographical boundaries free of any cultural, political, and ideological load that came to be attached to these terms in later ages. In the 1932 lecture course on the "Inception of Western Philosophy," Heidegger claimed:

We want to seek out the *inception* [*Anfang*] of Western [*abendländische*] philosophy ... Western philosophy takes its start [*Begin*] in the 6th century BCE, a small, relatively isolated, and purely self-dependent [*rein auf sich*

---

[37] The German source Heidegger provided is, Nietzsche, *Der Wille zur Macht. Gesammelte Werke* (Musarionausgabe). München 1920 ff. Bd. XIX, S. 360f., n. 1050 Heidegger [1929/1930], 73/ 110).

gestellten] (??) people of Greece.[38] They of course knew nothing of the 'Western" and the 'West' [*Abendland*]. These terms express first of all a geographical concept, drawing a boundary [*Abgrenzung*] against the East [*Morgenland*], the Oriental [*Orientalische*], the Asiatic [*Asiatische*].

Had the Greeks known something of this Western future, an inception of philosophy would never have come about. Rome, Judaism, and Christianity completely transformed and adulterated [*umgefälscht*] the inceptual – that is, Greek – philosophy. (Heidegger [1932], 1/1)

At this time, Heidegger had become somewhat reticent about the intellectual exchange of Greeks with other Asiatic peoples. Rather, he described the Greeks as a "relatively isolated" and "purely self-dependent" people. The double question marks that he added after this remark shows nevertheless his awareness that such a description was dubious and calls for more substantiation. Heidegger was discontent that the word "Western" (*abendländische*) has all along been treated as a historiological concept in connection with a neat lineage of history and culture, a lineage that has the Greeks as the starting point, with the Romans taking over the heritage, and with "Judeo-Christianity" carrying it forward and having fundamentally determined its character. This result is not what the Greeks could have foreseen and would have wanted because their inheritors contaminated and distorted the inceptual Greek philosophy. In *The Event*, a nonpublic text composed almost ten years afterward, Heidegger called post-Hellenic metaphysics "Occidental" (*occidentale*) philosophy and distinguished it from Western (*abendländische*) philosophy that enjoyed a unique bond with the Greek inception (Heidegger [1941/42a], 83/99; cf. Ma 2023).

In the lecture course "On the Essence of Truth" held in 1933/34, Heidegger drew attention to the Asiatic as an ontological force.

[T]he powers of destruction and ruination have their home *in* beings themselves; in struggle [*Kampf*] and through struggle they are only subdued and bound. And even then, these powers are still understood too negatively and not in the Greek sense, for these powers fundamentally break forth as the unbridled [*das Unbändige*], the unrestrained [*Zügellose*], the ecstatic and wild [*Rauschhafte und Wilde*], the raving [*Rasende*], the Asiatic [*Asiatische*]. We must be on our guard against devaluing these powers according to the Christian standards of evil and sin and thereby casting them into denial [*Verneigung*]. Neither does struggle, then, mean picking fights arbitrarily; struggle is the *innermost necessity* [*Notwendigkeit*] of beings as a whole and therefore the confrontation with and between the *primordial powers* [*Urmächten*]. What Nietzsche characterizes as the Apollonian and the Dionysian are the opposing powers of this struggle. (Heidegger [1933/34], 74/92)

---

[38] The mark (??) is from the original.

Heidegger suggested that we appreciate the import of the powers of gene-ration and preservation "in the Greek sense" precisely because these powers are "the unbridled, the unrestrained, the ecstatic and wild, the raving, the Asiatic." How to understand this *Greek Asiatic*? At the end of this long remark, Heidegger invoked Nietzsche's characterization of the Apollonian and the Dionysian. This well testifies to Nietzsche's influence on his writings on the Asiatic. In my view, Heidegger's *Greek Asiatic* is comparable to Nietzsche's "*Dionysiac Greeks*" (Nietzsche, [1870], 19). The "*Dionysiac Greeks*" were under the spell of a will for "the immense, for the multiple, the uncertain, the horrifying," and yet they had at disposal the mediation of the aesthetic necessity imposed by Apollo that sets them back to "measure," "simplicity," and "classification" (cited in Heidegger [1929/1930], 73/110). Similarly, the *Greek Asiatic* stands for the "unbridled," "unrestrained," "ecstatic and wild" ontological forces that break through and shatter the mediocracy and levelling down of beings, and yet these forces remain part and parcel of the "primordial powers" that struggle brings into confrontation out of necessity. The *Greek Asiatic* is the forgotten and yet much needed "*innermost necessity*" of Beyng as such. It is indispensable for the enactment of the other inception of Western philosophy. In this sense, the (Greek) Asiatic possesses a Beyng-historical signification and significance.

Hence, it is misleading to assume, as Richard Polt does, that the "Asiatic" serves as a reference to the "enemies" of the Greeks and to take this passage to be articulating the same "enmity" as when Heidegger "contrasts 'Asiatic' fatalism with Greek fate as vocation" (Polt 2019, 68).[39] The "Asiatic" in the 1933/34 lecture course "On the Essence of Truth" is definitely not downright negative, as Polt has presumed.

According to Heidegger, the received Aristotelian philosophy was a result of the interpretations by Islamic, Jewish, and Christian scholars – all of them immersed in monotheistic traditions. Such interpretations focus solely on constructing a neat system of concepts and principles. However, the originary power of life that the Asiatic indicates has been neglected. It is this unbridled power of life that made it possible for Beyng to break through and to reveal itself, and this "ecstatic and wild" ontological power lay at the foundation of early Greek thinking that initiated Western (*abendländische*) philosophy. We should neither neglect nor keep reticent about the Asiatic in the Beyng-historical sense that indicates the confrontation with and between the "primordial powers"

---

[39] The latter remark that Polt refers to appears in Heidegger [1934/35], 158/173. I discuss this passage and the second meaning of the Asiatic shortly.

out of historical necessity. It is this sense of the Asiatic that is concealed in Heidegger's enigmatic sayings such as the following:

> Toward the East [*Osten*]. Asia [*Asien*], Asia Minor, Ionia, Greece: It was the entire ancient world, from which the restless, magnificent, and superior soul, the soul that thinks of Being as a whole [*das ganze Sein*] – that is, the kingly soul —hoped for fulfillment. (Heidegger [1934/35], 186/204)

Most probably, Heidegger deployed such juxtapositions as Asia, Asia Minor, Ionia, Greece (all belonging to the East) in order to contrast them (and the futuristic *abendländische* philosophy that stems from them) with Islamic, Jewish, and Christian philosophy (what he called *occidentale* philosophy) that has distorted the original meaning of Being/Beyng. This antithesis between the Greek East and the Christian West resonates with Nietzsche's opposition between the Dionysian and the "Crucified." In the case of the Dionysian, "life itself, its eternal fruitfulness and recurrence, creates torment, destruction, the will to annihilation;" in the case of the "Crucified," by contrast, "suffering . . . counts as an objection to this life, as a formula for its condemnation" (Nietzsche 1968, 543).[40] The terms of this antithesis (in this case we could call it an opposition) diverge from that of the Dionysian and the Apollonian. The Dionysian obviously received preference over the Crucified. The former celebrates life while the latter condemns life.

From Heidegger's perspective, Christianity and the "Crucified" have completely downgraded and denied the ontological powers of destruction and ruination that nonetheless offers possibilities of generation and preservation. When these powers are missing, the vitality and promise for the happening of the Ereignis whereby Beyng shows itself are lacking. In order to welcome the other dawn of Beyng in the Evening-land (*Abendland*), the Asiatic in the Being-historical sense needs to be given due consideration.

From 1934 to 1937, Heidegger on several occasions touched on the early Greeks' "confrontation" (*Auseinandersetzung*) with the Asiatic. In his lecture course on Hölderlin's hymns "Germania" and "The Rhine" held in 1934/1935, which is his first sustained engagement with Hölderlin's poetizing, Heidegger claimed that Hegel's thinking was fueled by a new, creative, and repetitive execution of the originary thoughts (*Urgedanken*) of Heraclitus. Hölderlin, Nietzsche, and Meister Eckhardt were all under the sway of Heraclitus' thought. Following these claims, Heidegger turned to Heraclitus.

---

[40] In *Fundamental Metaphysical Concepts*, Heidegger also cited Nietzsche's remarks concerning the opposition of the Dionysian and the "Crucified" (Heidegger [1929/1930], 74/110–11).

The name Heraclitus is not the title for a philosophy of the Greeks that has long since run its course. Just as little is it the formula for the thinking of some universal world humanity in itself. Presumably, it is the name of a primordial power of Western-Germanic [*abendländisch-germanischen*] historical Dasein, and indeed in its first confrontation with the Asiatic. (Heidegger [1934/35], 118/134)

On this occasion, Heidegger spoke of the Germanic in the same breath as the Western. For him, all the inceptual German thinkers stood under the influence of the originary power of Heraclitus' thought. Among pre-Socratic Greek philosophers, Heraclitus of Ephesus (circa. 535–475 BCE) had the most intimate connection with the Eastern world. Being born in Ephesus situated at the Ionian coast of modern Turkey (part of Asia minor), he lived under the rule of the Persian King Darius (reign 521–486 BCE), who made Zoroastrianism the official teaching in the Persian Empire. Legend has it that Darius solicited Heraclitus' advice. Persian wisdom undeniably constituted the intellectual milieu for the formation of Heraclitus' intriguing philosophical ideas (and those of other Greek philosophers from Asia minor). It is not incidental that Heidegger picked him out as the typical Dasein who has wrestled with Asian thought.

Some pages further, when claiming that Hölderlin does not think the German word *Schicksal* (destiny) in terms of *Fatum* or *Fatalität*, Heidegger makes another remark containing two references to the Asiatic.

Precisely this Asiatic representation [*Vorstellung*] of destiny [*Schicksal*], as we may call it, is creatively overcome in Hölderlin's thinking. The first overcoming of the Asiatic fate [*Fatum*] was accomplished by the Greeks in an overcoming that, in the manner of its accomplishment, remains unrepeatable, and that occurred in unison with the emergence of this people through poetry, thinking, and statesmanship. Through the Greeks' knowing of μοῖρα and δίκη as such, what is thus named stands in the light of a Beyng that exceeds them. It loses its blind, exclusive character, and at the same time first takes on the aspect of that which is extraordinary, of an apportioning and determining that sets limits. (Heidegger [1934/35], 158/173)

Just before making this remark, Heidegger depicted the Asiatic notion of *Fatum* as "a will-less, unknowing progression amid the perpetual unfolding of some impassive fatality within the totality of beings that remain enveloped within themselves" and contrasted it with the Greek notion of μοῖρα (moira, usually translated as destiny), which, by standing in the light of a transcending Beyng, has rid itself of this blind and exclusive character (Heidegger [1934/35], 158/173). What matters is that the Asiatic notion of *Fatum* must undergo the Greek baptism in order to receive a new life from the light of Beyng. With reference to

Heidegger's relevant remarks, Charles Bambach describes the Asiatic accordingly:

> [Asia] stands as a name for the barbaric, the rootless, the allochthonic – those whose roots are not indigenous but who come from another place. For Heidegger, Asia comes to signify pure alterity, the otherness that threatens the preservation of the homeland. (Bambach 2003, 177)

Bambach rightly captures Heidegger's negative comportment toward the Asiatic that was overcome by the Greeks. Nevertheless, Asia/Asiatic is not merely an abstract notion signifying alterity because Heidegger did take into account the early encounter and interaction between the Greeks and other Asiatic peoples who inhabited the areas surrounding the Mediterranean Sea.

In the lecture course on Schelling's *Treatise on the Essence of Human Freedom* delivered in 1936, Heidegger remarked:

> For the great inception of Western philosophy, too, did not come out of nothing. Rather, it became great because it had to overcome [*zu überwinden*] its greatest opposite [*größten Gegensatz*], the mythical in general [*das Mythische überhaupt*] and the Asiatic in particular, that is, it had to bring it to the jointure [*Gefüge*] of a truth of Beyng [*Seyn*], and it was able to do this. (Heidegger [1936a], 146/252)

Citing this remark, J. L. Mehta commented that the Greeks had "overcome" Asia "as image" but they "never fully encountered and assimilated" it (Mehta 1992, 31). Bernasconi put forward a more negative evaluation by saying that Heidegger acknowledged the importance of the Asiatic for the Greeks "only so long as that was not the issue at hand" (Bernasconi 1995, 348). The word *Gegensatz* (and *Gegensätzlichkeit*), just as *Auseinandersetzung*, is polysemic and has a wide range of implications such as dichotomy, polarity, antithesis, and contradistinction. In this context, the Asiatic is described as the "greatest opposite," and this "greatest opposite" was overcome by the Greeks. Of course, it is difficult to decipher what could be entailed by Heidegger's supplementation of the mode of this overcoming as a matter of "bringing [the mythical/Asiatic] to the jointure of a truth of Beyng." On the one hand, this saying seems to forebode his later story about the Greeks' transformation of "Asia" (see Section 6) since before this citation Heidegger was talking about "transformation" as well, which means for him "to really bring about the hidden necessity of history" (Heidegger [1936a], 145/252). However, on the other hand, in the 1930s and 1940s Heidegger developed a negative view of "the mythical" (in the 1920s when discussing mythical Dasein he was not yet opposed to *das Mythische* as such). One remark from his *Ponderings* shares similar presumptions and seems to constitute a sequel to the one from 1936: "The most proximate decision: which

Western people is capable of developing and above all enduring *a completely other mode of thinking on the basis of Beyng,* over and against all metaphysics and myth [*Mythik*]" (Heidegger [1938/39a], 234/300–1). Both remarks stress the uniqueness of Beyng that serves as the yardstick for confronting all kinds of myth. The first remark from the lecture course on Schelling is made in connection with the first inception of philosophy in Greece, the Morning-land (*das Morgenland*). The second remark from the *Ponderings* is made in connection with the other inception of philosophy in the West, the Evening-land (*das Abendland*). The uniqueness of Beyng also functions as the standard for twisting free of the supposedly corrupted Occidental metaphysics (this history had not yet been unfolded when the first inception was initiated).[41]

In the 1932 lecture course, Heidegger stressed that "this way of Parmenides has nothing in common with myths [*Mythos*] and mysteries [*Mysterien*]" (Heidegger [1932], 86/113). In the *Event*, Heidegger repeatedly voiced a negative view of myth from the vision of the history of Beyng. He stressed that the "inhabited place of Da-sein lies outside of all historiology and technology, but also outside of all myths [*Mythen*] and prehistoric time" (Heidegger [1941/42a], 217/251). In conflating technology and myths, he was opposing the trend (maybe he had Cassirer in mind) that considered mysticism as a possible therapy for the disaster brought about by technology (cf. Heidegger [1941/42a], 75/89). Around that time, Heidegger does not seem to be concerned with the significance of providing an account of the "ontological constitution" of mythical Dasein (in a general sense) any more. Everything must be adjudicated according to the history (not historiology) of Beyng, and anything lying outside of it is either unhistorical or prehistoric.

On the other hand, Heidegger developed a positive account of the Greek word μῦθος. In the 1933/34 lecture course, Heidegger mentioned μῦθος as an older Greek word for the essence of language apart from λόγος and said that it is "not the word in which human beings give their account of things, but rather the word that gives them a directive [*Weisung*]" (Heidegger [1933/34], 91/116). According to him, "the originary λόγος of philosophy remains bound to μῦθος; only with the language of science is the bond dissolved (Heidegger [1933/34], 92/116). In a later lecture course on Parmenides, Heidegger said that the Greeks distinguished themselves from other peoples and call them barbarians, and that barbarism was opposed to "dwelling within μῦθος and λόγος" (Heidegger [1942/43], 70/103).

---

[41] Heidegger was not always consistent. In some places he said that inceptual thinking was not yet philosophy, and the latter only started with Plato (cf. Heidegger [1941/42], 51/63). However, in other more well-known works such as the *Contributions to Philosophy* of 1936–38 and *What is Philosophy* of 1955, he did not insist on this nuance.

Thus, we can discern that two meanings of "myth" are at play in Heidegger's own writings in a way similar to the duplicity of the Asiatic. One is the unhistorical "mythical in general" as related to the Asiatic – the Greeks' "greatest opposite" – which must be brought to the "jointure of a truth of Beyng," that is to say, it must be tempered by a modality of Beyng so that it can be overcome and transformed (Heidegger [1936a], 145–46/252). The other meaning of myth is most prominent when Heidegger discussed the myth (Mythos) of the allegory of the cave as the center of Platonic philosophy (cf. Heidegger [1933/34], 97/124). This meaning also comes across as the Greek μῦθος which belongs originarily with λόγος.

In the essay "Ways towards Discussion" prepared for the 1937 Descartes Congress held in Paris (which he failed to attend), Heidegger again referred to the confrontation with the Asiatic.

> When we reflect on the possible greatness and the standards set by Western "culture," we immediately remember the historical world of the early Greeks [*Griechentums*]. At the same time, we as easily forget that the Greeks did not become what they always already are through an encapsulation [*Verkapselung*] in their "space." It is only on the strength of the sharpest but creative confrontation with the most alien [*Fremdesten*] and most difficult [*Schwierigsten*] – the Asiatic – that this people grew up in the short course of its historical uniqueness [*geschich-tlichen Einmaligkeit*] and greatness. (Heidegger [1937], 20–21)

In the cited remark, Heidegger did admit that the ancestors of Western "culture" were not immune to the heterogeneous influences exerted by "Asiatic" traditions. What he highlighted, nevertheless, is the uniqueness and greatness of Greek thought that was able to attain maturity out of confrontation with the Asiatic. Meanwhile, he depicted the Asiatic as "the most alien and most difficult" that has stimulated the Greeks to become a unique and great people. In both remarks of 1936 and 1937, Heidegger praised the Greeks' creativity via which alone they achieved success in this confrontation. This resonates well with Nietzsche's ideas for whom the Greeks were "original inventors" "in a higher sense and a purer sphere," who had purified and sublimated whatever they had learnt from the Asiatic (Nietzsche [1873], 31/301).

Mehta quoted this passage from "Ways towards Discussion" and trans-lated *Auseinandersetzung* as "conflict and argument with" (Mehta 1992, 258). Although he did not offer a direct comment on the quotation, he cited Karl Löwith's remark from a "classic article" as a suitable elaboration of Heidegger's unsaid deliberation. Here is the cited remark: "this experi-ence of the essential difference between Orient and Occident has originally established and stamped the entire history of Europe," and the victory of the Greeks over the Persians was "the enduring beginning of European history" (cited in Mehta 1992, 258).

In general, Heidegger's remarks on the early Greeks' confrontation with the "Asiatic" in the 1930s were pervaded by a sense of resistance and antagonism that echoed his early comportment toward alien cultures in the 1910s and 1920s. The meaning of the "Asiatic" drastically differs from the Being-historical Asiatic that Heidegger drew attention to in the 1933/34 lecture course "On the Essence of Truth." If we call the latter the Greek Asiatic, we can call the former the *alien Asiatic*, the Asiatic that falls out of the history of Beyng. This parallels Nietzsche's distinction between the *"Dionysiac Greeks"* and the "Dionysiac barbarians" (Nietzsche [1872], 20/31).

4 The Russian "East" from out of the History of Beyng

A major part of this section is devoted to Heidegger's concern with Russianism (*Russentum*). This word – like other words such as *Deutschtum, Griechentum, Judentum,* and *Slaventum* – cannot be translated with a precisely corresponding English word. It can refer to the relevant people, to the character of the relevant nationality, and to the whole cultural-geographical world of the relevant nation. In general, I keep to the existing translations such as "Russianism" (occasionally as "Russianness"), "Germanism," "Jewishness," and "Slavicality" In order to disclose what is at stake with Heidegger's concern with Russianism, I first address Russia's complicated double identity using Fyodor Dostoevsky's (1821–1881) view as a cue.

Due to its special location intersecting with both Europe and Asia, Russia took up a complicated double identity. Before the reformation initiated by Peter the Great in the early eighteenth century, Russian tradition manifested a mixture of native polytheism, Byzantine culture (due to its conversion to Orthodox Christianity in 988), and a Mongolian-Tartarian legacy (due to two and half centuries' reign of the Mongolian Empire from the thirteenth to fifteenth century). Furthermore, according to some scholars such as Vladmir Stasov (1824–1906), ancient Asian traditions (Indian, Persian) exerted a significant influence on folk arts and myths in the rural areas in Russia. In particular, the style of Russian folk dance came from the Far East (cf. Figes 2003, xxix). Since the reformation by Peter the Great in the early eighteenth century, there appeared a rift between the old traditions preserved in the rural areas and the trend toward Europeanization brought about by that reformation, which gave rise to a Russian version of nihilism among the intelligentsia.

In his famous Pushkin Speech delivered on June 8, 1860, as well as in his *Diary of a Writer*, Dostoevsky attempted to mediate this rift generated by Russia's modernization by attending to its double identity. On the one hand, he advocated that the Russians "banish the slavish fear that Europe will call [them] Asiatic barbarians, and that it will be said that [they] are more Asiatic than Europeans" (Dostoevsky 1919, 1044). The Russians' eagerness to be identified as Europeans resulted in their loss of "spiritual independence" (Dostoevsky 1919, 1044). To remedy this situation, on the one hand, the Russians should revitalize and transform their "sick root," that is, Asia, their Asiatic Russia (Dostoevsky 1919, 1048). On the other hand, Europe is the "second mother" of the Russians. They should continue to take nourishment from Europe and remain grateful to her. However, their ultimate purpose is to create something like a "spiritual Egypt" for the Russians (Dostoevsky 1919, 1048). In my view, this means that they should create a new identity of the Asiatic Russia.

Dostoevsky's own literary works exhibited an integration of intellectual and spiritual sources from both Europe and Asia. He attached particular importance to a rediscovery of Russia's Asian root. When invoking the rich natural resources in Asia that had been much less explored than the hinterland of Africa, Dostoevsky compared Asia to America before its discovery by the Europeans.[42] He preached that, with the new expeditions to Asia, both the spirit and the forces of Russia would be regenerated, and this would be the most promising way for Russia to obtain independence.

> The moment we become independent, we shall find what to do, whereas during the two centuries with Europe we lost the habit of any work; we became chatterers and idlers. (Dostoevsky 1919, 1048)

When Moeller van den Bruck published German translations of Dostoevsky's works from 1907 to 1919, he presented Dostoevsky as a conduit for the original wisdom of the East. He predicted that "if some day evening comes to Western humanity and the German is at rest, only a Slavic mother could again bear Buddha or Jesus out of the Eastern world" (cited in Williams 1997, 79). Against the *Zeitgeist* of the decline of the West, what some European intellectuals expected from Dostoevsky are messages from (Russian) Eastern wisdom that could help save the world. This wisdom is Eastern in the sense of a synthesis of legacies from the Orthodox Church and the pervading influences from Asia (India, Mongolia, etc.).

---

[42] Some of Dostoevsky's observations were not immune from colonialist mentality.

Heidegger once mentioned his reading of Dostoevsky as a part of his "exciting years between 1910 and 1914" (Heidegger [1957], 10–11/56), and in an account from the *Ponderings* he set the starting point of his interest in Russia two years earlier: "My meditation [*Besinnung*] on *Russianism* began in 1908–1909, when I attempted, in my last year of secondary school, to learn Russian" (Heidegger [1939–41], 115/148). According to Petzet, for a long time a picture of Dostoevsky (and of Pascal) sat on Heidegger's desk (Petzet 1993, 120). Heidegger was familiar with Russian writers, either left-wing or right-wing. In a book review of 1910, he cited "Maxim Gorky the great vagabond" (Heidegger [1910], 35). In a footnote of *Being and Time*, he referred to Leo Tolstoy's *The Death of Ivan Ilyich* as an exemplification of "the disruption and breakdown of having 'someone die'" (Heidegger [1927], 495/254, note xii).[43] In a passage from the *Ponderings*, he said that the coining of the word "nihilism" and the conferral of its meaning "are connected to Turgenev who referred in this way to the Russian form of Western positivism" (Heidegger [1939–41], 38/49).[44] In the opening of the 1940 text entitled *Nietzsche: European Nihilism*, Heidegger commented that the word "nihilism" came into vogue via Turgenev, and his notion of nihilism entailed the idea that only what is perceptible to the senses is real and hence anything grounded on such values as tradition and authority is null. Heidegger added that this view was commonly called positivism (in the Western academia) (cf. Heidegger [1940], 3/2).

Following the previous comment, Heidegger referred to Dostoevsky's foreword to the Pushkin Speech and cited from it two paragraphs depicting the characteristics of Russian nihilists (Heidegger [1940], 3–4/1–2). These characteristics include restlessness, uprootedness, detachment from the folk heritage, distrust in the native soil, and a lack of any hope for Russia and for themselves. In opposition to some critics' evaluation of Pushkin's work as being primarily subject to Western influence, Dostoevsky identified it as a marvelous fruition of Pushkin's revitalization of Russian folk resources. In the same way, remaining true to the Russian native soil should be the way for the intelligentsia to overcome nihilism. Dostoevsky himself was regarded as an exponent of the intellectual movement called *pochvennichestvo* (почвенничество) that advocated returning to the native soil, that is, returning to Russia's folk heritage.

What is the character of Russia's folk heritage? For an ordinary European, Russia often came to mind with a stamp of "Asiatic." Clavdia Chauchat, the heroine from the Eastern reaches of Russia in Thomas Mann's 1924 novel *Magic Mountain*, was described in terms of "Asiatic." A French idiom goes

---

[43] For more discussions about Heidegger's connection with Dostoevsky and Tolstoy, see contributions in Love 2017, 31–94.

[44] The editor of GA 96 cites Turgenev's *Fathers and Sons* as an example.

like this, "Grattez le russe et vous verrez le tartare" (Scrape a Russian, then you find a Tartar).[45] Being "Asiatic" seemed to be an inborn nature of a Russian and was indigenous to anything related to Russia. For most European intellectuals, the disruptive forces that founded the Soviet Union are Asiatic. Such a sentiment finds reflection in Miguel de Unamuno's remark in *The Agony of Christianity* written in 1924:

> By way of rejoinder to all our questions we are told that both Christianity and Western or Graeco-Roman civilization will disappear together and that, via Russia and Bolshevism, another civilization, or whatever you care to call it, will emerge: an Asiatic, Oriental civilization, with Buddhist roots – a communist civilization. (Unamuno [1924], 66)

This view of Russia and Bolshevism as essentially interconnected with the Asiatic (or the Oriental) constituted the milieu in which Heidegger spoke of defending against the Asiatic. In the "Current Situation and Future Task of German Philosophy" of 1934, he observed:

> The true historical freedom of the peoples of Europe is the presupposition for the possibility that the West [*Abendland*] once again comes to itself spiritually and historically and ensures its fate [*Schicksal*] in the great decision of the earth against the Asiatic [*Entscheidung der Erde gegen das Asiatische*]. (Heidegger [1934], 333)

In 1936, Heidegger offered a two-fold solution for the salvation of Europe:

1. Keeping European people safe from Asiatic influences.
2. Overcoming the prevailing inner rootlessness and disintegration. [Heidegger [1936b], 679]

It is most probable that in these two citations the "Asiatic" referred to Russia (and Bolshevism) in view of Heidegger's well-known remark in *Introduction to Metaphysics* of 1935, where he said that Europe "lies today in the great pincers between Russia on the one side and America on the other" (Heidegger [1935], 40/40). In the latter place, the word "Russia" could be replaced by Bolshevism without change of meaning because of the negative implication of the word "pincers." Until the *Contributions to Philosophy* of 1936–38, Heidegger had not attempted to differentiate between the two terms of Russia and Bolshevism. When he started to do so, he used the word *Russentum* (to keep it apart from Bolshevism).

There is only one occurrence of the word *Russentum* in the *Contributions*. Heidegger used it to assert that Marxism had nothing to do with either

---

[45] Dostoevsky has cited this idiom for several times.

Jewishness (*Judentum*) or Russianness (*Russentum*). What follows this asser-
tion is intriguing: "if an undeveloped spirituality still lies dormant someplace,
then that place is the Russian people [*russischen Volk*]; Bolshevism is originally
West-oriented [*westlich*], a European possibility" (Heidegger [1936–38], 44/
54). The term *Russentum* often appears in Heidegger's *Ponderings*, mostly in
GA 96 from 1939–1941.

One of the central features of Heidegger's relevant observations in GA 96 is
the connection he made between Russianism and spirituality. By contrast,
Bolshevism is defined as "West-oriented" (*westlich*), having originated in
Europe and arisen from modern rational metaphysics. In other nonpublic
writings composed around the same period, Heidegger used the term "West-
oriented" to refer to Anglo-Franco thinking that privileged rationality as based
on self-certainty. This term is to be strictly distinguished from *Abendland* that
was promising of the other inception. For Heidegger, the *Abendland* is the
proper West and is central to the history of Beyng whereas *westlich* is derivative
and is related to modern rational metaphysics that evolved from a distorted
comportment toward Being/Beyng as beings (cf. Ma 2023). In *The Event*,
Heidegger commented that when Spengler used the word *Abendland*, he was
actually referring to "the demise of West-oriented civilization as 'culture'"
(Heidegger [1941/1942a], 81/96). In such cases, the term *westlich* (or *West*)
functions as a synonym of the Occidental, the latter term drawing more attention
to the origin of forgottenness of Being starting with the Roman-Latin tradition.

In GA 96, Heidegger devoted quite some space to differentiating Bolshevism
from Russianism. For him, Bolshevism – as "the unruly despotic-proletarian
Soviet power" (Heidegger [1939–41], 85/109) – amounted to "an authoritarian
state-capitalism, which has not the least to do with a compassionate socialism"
(Heidegger [1939–41], 104/134), and it was "only the configuration of *West-
oriented-modern* [*Westlich-neuzeitlichen*] thinking on the level of the closing
nineteenth century – the first decisive anticipation of the unrestricted power of
machination" (Heidegger [1939–41], 44/56–57).

These observations provided a more definitive configuration of Bolshevism in
Heidegger's mindset as the predecessor of machination. It is an integral part of the
lineage of "*West-oriented-modern* thinking." While enlisting Bolshevism with
the West-oriented and with modernity, Heidegger emphatically denied its connection to the Asiatic.[46] He remarked that Bolshevism "has nothing to do with the
Asiatic [*Asiatischen*] and even less to do with the Slavicality [*Slaventum*] of the
Russians [*Russen*] – or therefore with the basic Aryan essence [*Grundwesen*]"

---

[46] Although in the main Heidegger stressed that Bolshevism had nothing to do with the Asiatic, in
GA 96 he also spoke of the "Asiatic dullness of Bolshevism" (Heidegger [1939–41], 185/234).

(Heidegger [1939–41], 37/47). According to the received view at Heidegger's time, the Slavs were an inferior race that had degenerated from its Aryan origin because of blood mixture with the Asiatic peoples. Following the cited remark there arise two rhetorical questions: "What if Bolshevism destroyed Russianism? What if the identification of Russianism and Bolshevism completely guaranteed this destruction?" (Heidegger [1939–41], 37/47). We can sense what was at stake for Heidegger to keep Bolshevism at a remove from Russianism: For him, Russianism indicated something spiritual (though ambiguous) and pointed to a future that was promising of the salvation of the *Abendland* (West).

In another place, Heidegger observes that "Bolshevism, thoroughly un-Russian, is nevertheless a dangerous form of the distorted essence of Russianism and thus is a historical passageway" (Heidegger [1939–41], 97/125). Along the line of the digressive lineage after the first inception of Western philosophy, Heidegger here presented Bolshevism as "the distorted essence of Russianism" that is destined to pass away in due course. In GA 95, the second volume of *Ponderings*, one finds the remark:

> Why should not the purifying and securing of the race be destined one day to have as a consequence a great *mixture* [*Mischung*]: the one with the Slavs [*Slaventum*] (the Russians—on whom indeed Bolshevism has merely been forced and [Bolshevism] is [itself] nothing rooted [*nichts Wurzelhaftes*])? (Heidegger [1938/39a], 314/402)

Heidegger did not forget to mention his idiosyncratic distinction of the rootless Bolshevism from the Russians whom he aligned with the Slavs. By contrast, "Russianism has, in the unambiguousness of its brutality and stiffening, at the same time a *rooted source-region* [*ein wurzelhaftes Quellgebiet*] in its earth, which has predestined itself to be unique in the world" (Heidegger [1939–1941], 204/257; emphasis added). Heidegger's questioning in the foregoing citation from GA 95 thus continued:

> Would not the German spirit in its highest freshness and strength have to master here *a genuine darkness* [*ein echtes Dunkel*] and at the same time recognize it as its *root-ground* [*Wurzelgrund*]? (Heidegger [1938/39a], 314/402; emphasis added).

This remark broached the theme of what Heidegger in GA 96 called "a *confrontation* between *Germanism* [*Deutschtum*] and *Russianism* [*Russentum*]" (Heidegger [1939–41], 115/148). Heidegger conveyed an idea that is comparable to his observations on the early Greeks' confrontation with the Asiatic. The difference between these two rounds of confrontation is that Heidegger did not present Russianism outright as "the most alien and most difficult" in the same vein as the early Greeks' overcoming of the Asiatic.

Rather, he described Russianism as "a genuine darkness" and intimated that "the German spirit" should recognize Russianism as "its *root-ground*." How should we take this critical status that Heidegger ascribes to Russianism? The answer lies in the entangled connection between Germanism and Russianism that is to be "understood in terms of the history of Beyng" (Heidegger [1939– 41], 115/148). Heidegger did not offer any explication in concrete terms, but we can find some clues in a twelve-page text that is a part of a manuscript dated 1943/44, which was delivered to a small audience under the title "Poverty" on June 27, 1945.

According to Heidegger, the determination of spirit (*Geist*) and the spiritual in the current time is stuck in a mere negation (*Verneinung*) of matter and the material. The Greek word πνεῦμα, the Latin word *spiritus*, and the French word *esprit* contain more resources. The original meaning of *Geist* is "the effective power of enlightenment and wisdom, what the Greeks call σοφία" (Heidegger [1943/44], 4/874). With σοφία, there is no dualism of the spiritual and the material. In this connection Heidegger pointed to the divergence between the Occidental Roman Church and the Oriental Orthodox Church (*Ostkirche*) and claimed that it was with the latter that the "doctrine of Holy Sophia was unfolded" while the former followed the lead of Augustine's doctrine on trinity (Heidegger [1943/44], 4/874).[47] Heidegger affirmed that the doctrine of Holy Sophia remained alive in Russian mysticism (*Mystik*) "in a manner that we can hardly imagine," and he described "the efficacy of spirit as the all-pervading power of illumination [*Erleuchtung*] and wisdom (Sophia)" as "magical" (*magisch*) (Heidegger [1943/44], 4/874). After adding that "[t]he essence of the magical is as dark [*dunkel*] as the essence of the pneumatic," Heidegger turned to Jacob Böhme, "the theosophist and philosopher," who recognized that magical reality and took it be "the primal will" (*Urwillen*) (Heidegger [1943/ 44], 4/875). When Böhme's doctrine of the divine Sophia entered Russia in the seventeenth century, he was regarded as the holy father of the Orthodox Church, and his influence was renewed in the nineteenth century along with the import of Hegel and Schelling's philosophy that left an imprint on the thought of Vladimir Solovyov (Heidegger [1943/44], 4/875).[48] Hence, one of the things

---

[47] Heidegger stopped at mentioning that the Holy Spirit (Sophia) in the Orthodox Church often has a feminine image.

[48] In view of his friendship with Jaspers starting in 1920 when they met in Freiburg, Heidegger might have been informed by Alexandre Kojève's dissertation on Solovyov completed under Jaspers' guidance in 1924 (published in French in 1934). For instance, Kojève claims that "Schelling serves almost exclusively as [Solovyov's] model, and it is Schelling who resides at the root of nearly all his metaphysical ideas" (Kojève 2018, 19). This description has, in a way, reduced the originality of Solovyov's Sophiology, which was most influential in late imperial Russia.

Heidegger found to be special in the Russian tradition is this doctrine of Holy Sophia. In this context, he suggested that even materialism could not be purely material but came from a spiritual world.

In the light of this bond surrounding "spirit" and mysticism, Heidegger built up a constellation of Germanism versus Russianism. Insofar as the original significance of spirit as σοφία had been well preserved in Russian mysticism, Heidegger considered it as the "root-ground" of Germanism. From the vantage point of the history of Beyng, he observed that:

> reacquiring liberation of Russianism paves its way toward its history [*Geschichte*] (not "race") and an abyssal question-worthiness of the Germanism paves its way toward its history, whereby the history of both stems from the same concealed ground of an inceptual vocation [*Be-stimmung*]: to ground *the truth of Beyng* (as Er-eignis). (Heidegger [1939–41], 85/109–10)

Russianism must be liberated, probably from its outward "brutality and stiffening," and retrieve its status in the history of Beyng. Meanwhile, Germanism is also in need of questioning, a questioning that could touch its essential groundlessness so as to acquire a radical re-grounding. Both Russianism and Germanism share the vocation to ground the truth of Beyng. Having granted Russianism "the same concealed ground" of this inceptual vocation, Heidegger on this and some other occasions sang praises to Russianism for the promise of recuperation it could bring about. Along with such "sameness," Heidegger did not forget about the singularity of Russianism. He opposed the "*complete deracializing* [*vollständige Entrassung*] of peoples [*Völker*] through their being clamped into an equally built and equally tailored instituting of all beings," a deracializing that was engendered by machination. Such a deracializing would deprive peoples of their histories and make it impossible for such peoples of "preeminent historical power" as Germanism and Russianism to unite "precisely in their oppositionality: for example, the cognitive concept [*wissende Begriff*] and the fervor for meditation [*Leidenschaft der Besinnung*]" (Heidegger [1939–41], 44/56).[49] Obviously, "the fervor for meditation" is attributed to Russianism. This fervor lies behind Heidegger's attachment to Russianism.

In the 1935 *Introduction to Metaphysics*, Heidegger elucidated the "disempowering" of spirit, that is, "its dissolution, diminution, suppression, and misinterpretation" (Heidegger [1935], 47/34). He said that the source of this

---

[49] As early as in the 1915 lecture at Messkirch, Heidegger provided a definition of *Besinnung*: "Meditation [*Besinnung*] is the fathoming of sense [*Sinn*] down to its source and ground. The sense of something is its what, how, why, what-for" (Heidegger [1915a], 53).

"disempowering" came from Europe itself and was determined by the situation in the first half of the nineteenth century, but he also mentioned "earlier factors" without specifying them (Heidegger [1935], 48/34). In *Ponderings*, Heidegger provided some specifications of these earlier factors. He claimed that Descartes' rationalism had rejected "*all artificial 'mysticism' [Mystik] and 'myth' [Mythik]*" while true mysticism and myth abounded in the earth of Russianism (Heidegger [1938/39a], 133/173). He also remarked that German Idealism grasped both "the mechanicism of West-oriented thinking" and "the irrationality of 'organic' life," and it brought rationalism to its ultimate fruition by revealing its metaphysical underpinnings (Heidegger [1939–41], 8/9).

However – as Heidegger observed in the *Introduction to Metaphysics* – in the first half of the nineteenth century, German idealism was said to "collapse," which according to Heidegger was an inapt description. For him, "it was not German idealism that collapsed, but it was the age that was no longer strong enough to stand up to the greatness, breadth, and originality of that spiritual world" (Heidegger [1935], 48/35). In accordance with Heidegger's diagnosis of the time, after the "collapse" of German Idealism as occasioned by the "disempowering" of spirit, what dominated German philosophy was "the cognitive concept." Germanism was unable to properly appropriate its own mystic and spiritual tradition as exemplified in such figures as Jacob Böhme, who had exerted influences on Russian mysticism in both an earlier and a recent century.

Hence, a confrontation between Germanism and Russianism out of the history of Beyng is called for, a confrontation in which, via "originary and thoughtful pronouncement of the abyss of Beyng, a pronouncement that is over and done with all metaphysics and all Christian pursuit of culture," the "undisclosed mystery [*Geheimnis*] of Russianism (not of Bolshevism) can be bestowed and grounded as such" (Heidegger [1939–41], 438/48).[50] For Heidegger, the Beyng-historical weight that should be given to Russianism was integrally bound up with the project of twisting free of past metaphysics that has almost completely abandoned its mystic and spiritual tradition. In view of the urgency of this task, Heidegger regretted that the Germans knew nothing about Russia though the Russians were well versed in German metaphysics and poetry. It was of supreme urgency to know who the Russians are.

Heidegger lamented a "great, precipitous, *historiographical assault* upon *Russia*, a limitless, ongoing exploitation of *raw materials* for the intricacies of the 'machine'" (Heidegger [1938–40], 101/120). He admonished more directly that "we not assail it technologically and culturally and ultimately annihilate [*vernichten*] it," and he added a note indicating

---

[50] Heidegger normally reserved such terms as *Geheimnis* for Greek and German thinking.

what *vernichten* means: "not to wipe out physically, nor even defeat militarily, but to deprive it of its own concealed essence through renewed and radical implication in the machination to which we ourselves have fallen prey" (Heidegger [1938–40], 100/119).

What is more tragic than militarily defeating or physically eradicating Russia is to destroy its "concealed essence" by entangling it into the pervasive commandeering machination. Instead, "we" should "set [Russia] free for *its* essence and open up for it the expanse of its ability to suffer the essentialness of an essential saving of the earth" (Heidegger [1938–40], 100/119).

Heidegger has repeatedly claimed that Bolshevism is "nothing Asiatic," but would he disown any connection to the Asiatic as regards Russia? Once he asked himself, "*Russia* is not Asia or Asiatic and yet belongs just as little to Europe. What then is it?" (Heidegger [1939–1941], 134). Heidegger wanted to grant a unique place to Russia in the constellation of the history of Beyng, but the question remains: would it be possible to eradicate any historiological connection with the Asiatic/Asia that had shaped the (double) identity of Russia? One could argue that what Heidegger was concerned with is nothing else than a Russianism that he had invented himself, which is purely conceptual, or purely Beyng-historical, in the way in which his anti-Semitism is a Beyng-historical anti-Semitism.[51] However, we can discern moments when Heidegger overlooked his own efforts at insulating Russianism from the Asiatic. This comes across in a passage from *Metaphysics and Nihilism*, which is a part of the *Black Notebooks*. He wrote in relation to Americanism: "Ghastlier than any Asiatic wildness is this uprooted morality, which extends to unconditional hypocrisy," whereupon he asked whether it could be recognized that all ghastliness – that is, the frightening, intensely unpleasant, and disagreeable – lies in Americanism and "not *at all* in Russianism" (Heidegger [1938/39b], 150).

For Heidegger, "Americanism is the historically identifiable phenomenon of the unconditional conversion of modern times into devastation [*Verwüstung*]" (Heidegger [1939–1941], 204/257). In comparison, "Russianism is too indigenous [*bodenständig*] and antirational [*vernunftfeindlich*] for it to be capable of taking over the historical vocation of the devastation" (Heidegger [1939–1941],

---

[51] For Heidegger's alleged Beyng-historical anti-Semitism, compare Trawny 2017. In my view, if one could speak of a Beyng-historical Russianism in Heidegger's thought, it is more concretely anchored than a Beyng-historical anti-Semitism or a Beyng-historical East Asia as he constructed in the 1953/54 "A Dialogue on Language" (although Heidegger himself, to be sure, did not use the epithet of "Beyng-historical"). Presumably, he was better informed of the complicated traditions of his neighbor country Russia than those of the Far East.

204/257–58).[52] Clearly, Americanism was more integral with the West-oriented than Bolshevism (or Russianism in this case). The word "antirational" echoes the "Asiatic wildness" from the previous quote. Here, Heidegger conveyed a different evaluation of Russianism in attributing to it the descriptor of "antirational." This contrasts with his attribution of the descriptor of "irrational" (*Irrationale*) to it when discussing the "unique encounter in juxtaposition and succession" of Germanism and Russianism, and he qualified the distinction of "rational" and "irrational" as "superficial" and "sham" (Heidegger [1938/39a], 314/403).

It seems that Heidegger did not forget the deeply ingrained assumption of Russia as Asiatic, which assumption was shared by most Europeans. We find an interesting remark in GA 95, the second volume of the *Ponderings*:

> And how should this future of the West [*Abendland*] – which alone would be equal once again to the Asiatic [*Asiatischen*] – not proceed along at the margin of its *greatest danger* – that that unification of Germanism and Russianism would amount only to the most extreme intensification of the consummation of modernity – that the inexaustibility of the Russian earth would be taken up into the irresistibility of German planning and ordering. (Heidegger [1938/39a], 314/403)

From Heidegger's perspective, the confrontation between Germanism and Russianism should not remain at the surface, that is, it should not be treated as merely political and military affairs. This would more so be the case if Russianism were implicitly identified with Bolshevism. Neither should it be considered to be, at the intellectual level, a matter of integration of "the cognitive concept and the fervor for meditation" (Heidegger [1939–41], 44/56). Something more should come out of this confrontation. Furthermore, Heidegger was very much concerned that the rich resources of the Russian earth should not be subject to unrestrained planning and ordering of machination. The "earth" has a Beyng-historical dimension. As Heidegger remarked on another occasion:

> The history of the earth of the future is reserved within the essence of Russianism, an essence that has not yet been set free for itself. The history of the world is a task assigned to the Germans for *mindfulness* [*Besinnung*]. (Heidegger [1938–40], 91/108).

---

[52] Following this quote, Heidegger asserts that "what would be required is a *rationality* [*Vernünftigkeit*] complete to the highest degree and calculating everything, and this could also be called "spirituality [*Geistigkeit*]. Only such 'spirit' is equal to the historical task of devastation" (Heidegger [1939–1941], 204/258).

It seems that Heidegger would not stop at an opposition between rationality and spirituality. What he called for is a "spirit" that integrates rationality and spirituality.

Behind the surface confrontation between Germanism and Russianism is concealed a confrontation of the West (*Abendland*) with the Asiatic. The latter is the most fundamental and most decisive confrontation in the Beyng-historical sense. It should not proceed at the margin but rather must engage the very danger lying at the heart of the entangled relation of Germanism and Russianism, one which Heidegger formulated as a relation between the earth and the world. In a nutshell, behind Heidegger's elaboration of Russianism in connection with Germanism is an even deeper – and abyssal – relation of the West (*Abendland*) with the Asiatic. The Asiatic exceeds what Heidegger has presented as Russianism, and it is what Heidegger hoped to keep in play via the confrontation between Germanism and Russianism. In other words, there is more to Heidegger's version of Russianism than he has rendered to fit neatly into the constellation of the history of Beyng.

However, Heidegger was far from willing to disclose all the subtle shades of his considerations at once. That is probably why he rarely used the word "Asiatic" in relation to Russia in the late 1930s and early 1940s. On one occasion, he used the phrase of "*Asiatic* East" with an emphasis on "Asiatic": "For us to kindle the flames of this struggle [that is, the struggle of the Germans 'over their most proper *essence*'], what suffices is neither opposition against the West [*Westen*] nor opposition against the *Asiatic* East [*asiatischen Osten*]" (Heidegger [1938/39a], 9/11).

More often, Heidegger turned to the word "East" [*Ost*] to refer to both the surface Russia – that is, Bolshevik Russia as part of machination and the planetary – and the concealed Russia/Russianism that embodied a rich mystic and spiritual tradition. "Insofar as technology and communism assault the West [*Westen*] out of the East [*Osten*], in truth the West [*Westen*] is assaulting the West [*Westen*] in an uncanny self-annihilation of its own powers and intentions" (Heidegger [1939–41], 219/276).

Here, the East refers to the surface Russia under the regime of the Soviet Union. According to Heidegger, Bolshevism originated in the Occidental metaphysics with a distorted comportment to Being. In this sense, he envisioned the current East–West conflict as in fact a West–West conflict that would be a self-annihilation (and a consummation of modernity as well). On the other hand, we find him making the following claim:

> Besides its public aspect, history always also has its concealed one.

> Consummated metaphysics will find the fitting site for its rebirth in Russianism. From there someday, as a counterprojection [*Gegenwurf*], this metaphysics will come to meet the inception. (Heidegger [1939–41], 219/276)

This sounds rather laudatory of Russianism. For Heidegger, a new inception of Western (*abendländische*) philosophy would be possible via a twisting free of past metaphysics, that is, to let it play out its uttermost destructive possibilities, or, alternatively speaking, to leave it to its own devastation (*Verwüstung*) in consummation. During the most intense years of World War II from 1939 to 1945, Heidegger secretively searched for a forgotten source of "Eastern" wisdom in Russianism as an integral part of the heritage of the Oriental Orthodox Church privileging σοφία (Sophia). Beneath the surface conflict between the East – which is in fact a projection of the West (*Westen*) in the historiographical sense – and West, Heidegger advocated a much deeper confrontation with Russianism such that, with the consummation of metaphysics, a new inception of Western (*abendländische*) philosophy would be enacted in Russianism, that is, the East. That is to say, a re-enactment of the Abendland – the West in the Beyng-historical sense – would in turn be seen as a projection of the East. This is the way in which we could understand his diction of "counter-projection." As Heidegger affirmed in another place:

> The "Abendland" is a historical concept which determines the essential history of the Germans (and also determines their origination [*Herkunft*]) out of a confrontation with the Eastern [*Morgenländischen*]; but this confrontation does not collapse [*verfällt*] into the West-land [*Westländische*]. (Heidegger [1939–1941], 217/274)

That the confrontation between Germanism and Russianism does not collapse into the West-land suggests that it would end up in the East-land – in a way, a Beyng-historical East.

There is yet a different sense to the "East." For Heidegger, all the areas on this planet were subject to planetarism. Europe is a planetary concept covering "evening and morning, West [*Westen*] and East [*Osten*], and indeed even transferring the weight to the *land of the morning* [*Morgenland*], the East" (Heidegger [1939–41], 217/274). The "East" in this context refers to Russia that is under the sway of modernity, machination, and Bolshevism. Heidegger also observed:

> All the modern things – also all the things of the East [*das des Ostens*] – belong to metaphysics; no renewal of the past, no radicalization of what is already-standing and pressing could here prepare the passing-by. (Heidegger [1942–1948], 112)

With the expansion of modernity, the "East" became part of the planetary, which stems from traditional Occidental metaphysics. A wholesale devastation instead of piecemeal renewal and supplementation is called for in order to have the other inception enacted. On another occasion, Heidegger more directly claimed: "Occident [*Occident*] and Orient [*Orient*] must first undergo devastation out of the planetary" (Heidegger [1941/42a], 82/98). What was at stake here was a vision from the history of Beyng:

> The concept of the West [*Abendland*], as understood in the history of Beyng, needs to be delimited against the historiological-geographical concept, which remains oriented to morning and evening in the sense of East [*Osten*] and West [*Westen*] and thus in a certain way does indeed still refer to the Beyng-historical and metaphysical region. (Heidegger [1941/42a], 82/97)

Heidegger tended to distinguish the *Abendland* in the Beyng-historical sense from (East and) West in the historiological-geographical sense. Although East and West are bound up with the metaphysical region, they have the promise of being transformed into Beyng-historical notions after the devastation (or, against the devastation). Heidegger was deploying two meanings of the East: the East as subject to planetarism and a sort of Beyng-historical East that has a similar function as the Beyng-historical Asiatic as discussed in Section 3. The Beyng-historical East – the typical case being the Russian East – also bears a connection to Greece via the notion of σοφία and mysticism.

5 Appropriation of the *Zhuangzi* in the 1940s

Toward the late 1930s and early 1940s, with the political and social tensions in Germany increasing every day, more intellectuals turned to Asian philosophy, in particular Daoism, for an alternative outlook of the world. Around 1938, with the aid of Heinrich Zimmer, a specialist of Asian studies, Karl Jaspers began to read and study classical texts from the Far East (cf. Salamun 2022, 85–86).[53] This encounter finally led to the formulation of Jaspers' idea of the Axial Age in the late 1940s. While in exile in Denmark in 1938, Bertold Brecht composed the ballad "Legend about the Origin of the Book *Daodejing* on Laozi's Way into Emigration." Petzet reported that Heidegger "loved" this poem and presumed that Heidegger might recognize himself in it (Petzet 1993, 217). In the famous drama *The Good Person of Szechwan* (Sichuan), which was premiered in Zürich on February 4, 1943, Brecht showed concern with the suffering of usefulness (*das Leiden der Brauchbarkeit*) building on relevant passages from chapter 4 of the *Zhuangzi*. What he used is the translation by Richard Wilhelm with slight modifications (Brecht 1989, 241; cf. Wilhelm [1912], 35).

It can be said that Heidegger was subject to this second wave of turning to the Far East around that time when the world was set into a whirlpool of wars and

---

[53] As can be evidenced by the two dissertations that he supervised, one by Kojève on Solovyov (completed in 1924; cf. Kojève 2018) and the other by Kitayama on Buddhist metaphysics (completed in 1930; cf. Kitayama 1934), Jaspers' interest in the East seemed to surface much earlier.

conflicts. In an essay entitled "The Uniqueness of the Poet," he cited the whole of chapter 11 from the *Daodejing* (Heidegger [1943b]).[54] In November 1944, Freiburg was destroyed by the bombardment of the Allied force. Soon afterward, Heidegger obtained the permission to retreat to his hometown Messkirch to sort out his manuscripts. His letters to his wife Elfride (and to his brother Fritz) during this period provided relevant clues for deciphering his thoughts that led up to his citation from the *Zhuangzi* toward the end of his essay "Evening Conversation" dated May 8, 1945. He confessed to his wife that he took this retreat as an opportunity to "concentrate upon the essential and reflect on the paths," which was nevertheless disturbed by concerns with daily needs (*Not*) (Heidegger 2008, 183/228). With this, Heidegger contrasted "the innermost need [*die innerste Not*] of history and the West [*Abendland*] . . . [that] saps and strains one in quite a different way from social affliction and human suffering" (Heidegger 2008, 183/228).

In the meantime, Heidegger sensed the "necessity" (*Notwendigkeit*) of a simple saying because "our language only applies to what has been up to now"; by "our language," Heidegger referred to "the merely scholastic and scholarly" that "would unexpectedly intrude and hinder or warp the simple and essential (Heidegger 2008, 182/228; 190/238). Heidegger thus elaborated on his new discovery:

> I suddenly found a form of saying, which I would never have dared use, if only because of the danger of outwardly imitating the Platonic dialogues [*Dialoge*]. I'm working on a "conversation" [*Gespräch*] – actually I have the "inspiration" – I must call it this, several ["conversations"] in the meantime. In this way, poetizing and thinking saying has attained a primordial unity, and everything flows along easily and freely. (Heidegger 2008, 187/235)

This is a rare occasion on which Heidegger provided an account for the origin of his trilogy of *Country Path Conversations* composed in 1944/1945. Heidegger might be drawing on the discursive form of "conversation" (*Gespräch*) as is commonly seen in the *Zhuangzi* instead of the more abstract Platonic dialogues (*Dialoge*).

Another letter dated October 8, 1946 (one year later) to his brother Fritz evidenced the availability of the Chinese source during Heidegger's sojourn in Messkirch in 1945. In that letter, Heidegger asked Fritz to bring some books he kept in Messkirch to his cabin at Todtnauberg (close to Freiburg).

> I don't need [the book] *Aristoteles* by Christ; instead, [I need] volume one of the fifth printing of *Fragments of Presocratics* and the two yellow volumes of

---

[54] For a detailed discussion of Heidegger's encounter with the *Daodejing*, compare Ma 2008, chapter 6.

Chinese philosophy *Lao-tse* [*Laozi*] and *Dschuang*-tse [*Zhuangzi*].
A Chinese, who listened to [my lectures] for years, would like to complete
the translation of Lao-tse in Freiburg with my help.[55] (Heidegger 2016, 139)

The "Chinese" most probably refers to Shih-Yi Hsiao 蕭师毅, who is best
known for his collaboration with Heidegger to translate several chapters from
the *Daodejing* into German in the summer of 1946 (cf. Ma 2008, 153–57).
Meanwhile, it is notable that Heidegger's turn to East Asia was often accom-
panied by an ever-deepened exploration of pre-Socratic thinkers who initiated
the first inception of Western philosophy.

The letter to his wife dated March 2, 1945 was the earliest occasion on which
Heidegger invoked "the short conversation" from the *Zhuangzi* that he cited in
his proper philosophical writing.

> I often now think of Grillparzer's comment on modernity: "From humanity
> indeed through nationality to bestiality."[56] However, this process as a whole
> is already proceeding in the subjecti[vi]ty wherein humanity has lost the
> appropriate relation to the unneeded [*Unnötigen*], indeed perhaps had never
> attained it. To be sure, this is difficult or even impossible to grasp for a world
> of achievement and work, of power and success, which is why this must
> vanish too; but it won't have vanished by the day after tomorrow and in
> predictable time. Concerning the essence of the unneeded (it is what I mean
> by "Being" [*Sein*]) I found of late the short conversation [*das kurze
> Gespräch*] between two Chinese thinkers, which I transcribe for you.
> (Heidegger 2008, 187/234)

Heidegger's observations are rather compact. What is most notable is his conflation of the "unneeded" (*Unnötigen*) with his fundamental word of Being (*Sein*). In
another letter to his brother Fritz three days later, that is, March 5, 1945,
Heidegger again touched on this conversation from the *Zhuangzi*. This letter

---

[55] The first book Heidegger mentioned in his letter is Wilhelm von Christ, *Aristotelis Metaphysica
recognovit W. Chris.* Lipsiae in aedibus B. G. Teubneri, 1886.

[56] Franz Seraphicus Grillparzer (1791–1872) was an Austrian writer and dramatist as well
as a devoted conservative patriot who despised petty nationalism. The famous epigram
that Heidegger cited arose as Grillparzer's immediate response to the acts of cruelty in
Italy in 1849.

> The way of modern formation [*Bildung*],
> Leads from humanity
> Through nationality
> To bestiality.

In the "Supplements" to the "Evening Conversation," Heidegger cited the same epigram without
mentioning Grillparzer by name (Heidegger [1945], 159/243). In the main text of "Evening
Conversation," Heidegger posed criticisms of narrowly conceived nationalism (Heidegger
[1945], 153–154/234–237).

started with saying that he had waited for Fritz to come to Messkirch but Fritz did not arrive. That was followed by an enigmatic observation:

> The difference between beings and Beyng becomes even more unfathomable [*rätselhafter*]. Perhaps this name is already unsuitable and with it [there appears] the way [*Hinsicht*] and presupposition [*Ansatz*] of interpretation [*Deutung*].
>
> The brief conversation [*das kleine Gespräch*] between two Chinese thinkers (Asia! [*Asien*]) certainly gives you happiness. (Heidegger 2016, 123)

In these two letters, one to his wife and one to brother, Heidegger explicitly connected the "unneeded" to Being and to his idea of the ontological difference between "beings and Beyng," though he regretted that humanity had never attained an adequate relation to the unneeded.

Heidegger's transcription of this "brief conversation" was retained in the case of his letter to his brother but not in the case of the letter to his wife. The cited passage from the *Zhuangzi* was not included in the 1910 Buber edition, and Heidegger did not mention the source. In the transcript, however, Heidegger followed Wilhelm's version almost verbatim, including the short subtitle which Wilhelm added: "The Necessity of the Unneeded" (*Die Notwendigkeit des Unnötigen*) (Heidegger 2016, 124; cf. Wilhelm 1912, 203–4). In the "Evening Conversation," which is the third of the trilogy of *Country Path Conversations,* Heidegger quoted the same passage, but he replaced the names of Huizi and Zhuangzi with "The one" and "The other" respectively (Heidegger [1945], 156/ 239). By leaving out the proper names, Heidegger presumably intended to create a polysemous space for the East/Asia. The relevant passage, which is from chapter 26 of the *Zhuangzi*, reads as follows:

> The one [Huizi] said, "You talk about the unneeded."
>
> The other [Zhuangzi] said, "One must first know the unneeded [*das Unnötige, wuyong* 无用]; Then can someone talk with him/her about the useful [*vom Nötigen*]. The earth is so wide and huge, but in order to stand the human uses as little a patch as one can set one's feet on. If, however, directly next to one's feet a crevice were to open up that dropped down into the underworld, could one still make use [*zu etwas nütze*] of that little patch on which he/she stands?"
>
> The one [Huizi] said, "It would be useless [*Er wäre ihm nichts mehr nütze*]."
>
> The other [Zhuangzi] said, "Then the necessity of the unneeded [*die Notwendigkeit des Unnötigen*] becomes evident." (Heidegger [1945], 156/239)[57]

---

[57] "[T]he necessity of the unneeded" translates the phrase *wuyong zhi weiyong* 无用之為用 in Chinese. Zhuangzi indicated the way in which what is considered useless makes possible what is regarded as directly useful.

The word of *Notwendigkeit* (necessity) carries multiple layers of connotations. It contains the word *Not* that means "need," but *"Not"* also indicates trouble or distress and hence can also be translated as "plight" on some occasions. *Notwendigkeit* also contains the word *wendig*, which means "flexible," and one of its literal meanings is *geeignet*, that is, suitable or appropriate. This implies that the "necessity" (of the unneeded) at issue here is to respond to the specificity of the situation. This kind of responsive necessity can be revealed in the relation between the little patch upon which one's feet can be set and the earth surrounding it. It is not a logically binding relation. However, precisely this unobtrusive and yet silently supporting necessity has been "cast out into a desolate abandonment." Hence, Heidegger calls on everybody to learn to "know the plight [*Not*] in which everywhere the unneeded [*Unnötige*] must still persevere" (Heidegger [1945], 155/237). His appropriation of the *Zhuangzi* can be well appreciated in the light of his more explicit claims made in the letters to the two persons closest to him.

We have seen that in his letters in March 1945, Heidegger explicitly connected the "unneeded" to Being and to his idea of the ontological difference between "beings and Beyng." It is interesting to notice that in some writings of the late 1930s, Heidegger was already discussing Being/Beyng in terms of the unneeded or the ne-cessity (*Not-wendige*). For example, in *Mindfulness*, he wrote "that humanity can do without Beyng, that s/he can disregard Beyng, that Beyng does not heed this: the wholly un-needed [*das ganz Un-nötige*] which thus is the ground for the lack of distress [*Notlosigkeit*]" (Heidegger [1938/39a], 118/139). In a passage from his *Ponderings*, he explains:

> Beyng, grasped as plight [*Not*], does not mean something which is necessary [*not-tut*]—for example, in the idealistic sense of a necessary condition [*benötigten Bedingung*] for the grasp of beings as objects. Beyng "is" and only Beyng originarily "is"—it is "not necessary" [*es »tut nicht not«*]—but, instead *compels* [*nötigt*]; Beyng does not correspond to some sort of "needing" [*Bedürfen*]—but is rather the abyss of all essential dispositions which, badly disposed, flee into the mistaken form of mere needs [*Bedürfnisse*] and as such claim the human being. (Heidegger [1938/39a], 197/254)

Clearly, Heidegger attempted to twist free the traditional conception of Beyng as a necessary condition for grasping beings as objects and to formulate a new notion of Beyng that is "not necessary" but rather is an accident – to put it differently, a notion that entails no causal relations between Beyng and beings. It is the abyssal ground (or lack of ground) for the intelligibility and usefulness of beings. A few pages later in the same volume, Heidegger directly spoke of Beyng as the accident for every being.

If the human *essence* decreases itself, that is, falls into the distorted essence of the unfastening from Beyng, then what in-creases is the arrogance of the "real" human being, the one "standing with both feet in reality." Why should his/her successes not persuade him/her that there are no accidents and that everything is merely a matter of "will"? But what if Beyng were the accident for every being, because Beyng is the only ne-cessity [*das allein Not-wendige*]—the plight [*Not*] itself? (Heidegger [1938/39b], 201–2/259)

It is not impossible that the phrase "standing with both feet in reality" contains an implicit reference to the short conversation from the *Zhuangzi*. Humans are self-assured about the fact that they stand firmly on solid ground, treating beings in terms of cause–effect relations and disregarding the things that seem to be short of such relations and appear to be useless. As is mentioned, the word *Notwendigkeit* has an inner connection with *Not*: Beyng could be grasped as plight (*Not*), which is induced by the abandonment of beings by Beyng. However, one must think through this plight, which would hopefully lead one to turn away from the plight – this is one of the literal meanings of *notwendig*, that is, *die Not abzuwenden* – from within this plight. Only with the occurrence (*Ereignis*), which is the accident for every being, can the usefulness of any entity be brought to dawn on the human being.

In "Poverty," Heidegger formulated an argument that identifies his understanding of *Notwendigkeit* with freedom, drawing on the meaning of the word *Not* as "need." According to him, "the needed [*Nötig*] is that which arises out of and through need [*Not*]," and "the essence of need is compulsion [*Zwang*], following the basic meaning of the word" (Heidegger [1943/44] 6/878). By contrast, the unneeded "is what does not arise out of need, that is, is what does not arise out of compulsion, but out of the freeing [*aus dem Freien*]"; and, thus, "originarily and properly 'the freeing' means to safeguard [*schonen*], to let something rest in what is its own essence through sheltering [*Behüten*]" (Heidegger [1943/44] 7/878). Consequently, "[f]reedom is the need being turned around" (alternatively speaking, freedom is the unneeded), and necessity in the sense of unneeded sways "only in freedom and in its safeguarding freeing" (Heidegger [1943/44] 7/878). In this light, necessity is not the opposite of freedom as traditional metaphysics has assumed, but rather, freedom in its essence is truly ne-cessity, that is, the turning around of need (*Not-wendigkeit*). Furthermore, Heidegger defines "beyng-poor" (*Armseyn*) as "being deprived of nothing except the un-needed, that is, being deprived of nothing except the freeing-liberating [*das Freie-Freiende*]" (Heidegger [1943/44] 7/878). Finally, Heidegger equalized the "liberating" with Beyng that lets beings rest in their essence and safeguards all beings (Heidegger [1943/44] 8/878).

In view of these writings from the late 1930s and the early 1940s, we can see that Heidegger's "use/abuse" (*Vernutzung*) – to use his own word in the remark of 1954 that I cite in the Introduction (Heidegger 2020, 109) – of the *Zhuangzi* pivots significantly upon his radical renovation of fundamental notions and themes of traditional Western philosophy.

After considering Heidegger's appropriation of the *Zhuangzi* that went along with the second wave of interest in East Asia starting in the late 1930s, can we claim without reservation a uniquely "Daoist" turn in Heidegger's thinking?[58] Before we venture an answer to this question, we should not neglect the fact that the "Evening Conversation" is set in "a prisoner of war camp in Russia," and it opens with a long exchange about "something healing [*das Heilsame*]" that rests on "what is inexhaustible of the self-veiling expanse that abides in these forests of Russia" (Heidegger [1945], 132/205). At the same time, the expanse delivers the essence of both conversation partners "into the open [*ins Offene*] and at the same time gathers it into the simple" (Heidegger [1945], 132/205). This is followed by attention to the devastation (*Verwüstung*), which means that "everything—the world, the human, and the earth—will be transformed into a desert [*Wüste*]" (Heidegger [1945], 136/211). In fact, Heidegger's concern with the Russian East sets the overall tone of the "Evening Conversation." The "Conversation" was composed against the constant conflicts of East (*Osten*, that is, Russia) and West (*Westen*), and Heidegger's two sons were missing on the Russian front. Concerning the latter, Heidegger said in a letter of April 3, 1945, "Thinking about the two of them has given me a strange strength in writing the Conversation" (Heidegger 2008, 188/235). Hence, Heidegger's concern with the "East" in that period cannot be reduced to the Asian East because a concern with the Russian East remained central to the "Conversation" (of course, a reduction in the reverse direction is equally implausible, since Heidegger's concern with the Russian East was not isolated from a concern with the "Asiatic"). In what can be viewed as an afterword to the "Conversation," Heidegger writes:

> In what is essential [*eigentlichen*] I must probably tread the path alone, without making anything special of this solitude. I have the clear feeling that in Messkirch it would become "natural" and the work would be part of the growth of the native soil [*Heimatboden*] precisely because it is growing into what is universal and is becoming something that could creatively incorporate "the East" [*den Osten*] within its unfathomable [*rätselhaften*] essence beyond the immediately apparent "political" conflict. I often think it

---

[58] On two other occasions in the early 1960s, Heidegger again cited from the *Zhuangzi* (Heidegger [1960], Heidegger [1962a]). On the first occasion, he cited the story concerning the way in which Carpenter Qing carved out a bell-stand of superb quality; On the second occasion, he cited another conversation between Zhuangzi and Huizi about the useless tree. For a discussion of these citations, see Ma and van Brakel 2014.

can be no accident that Jörg and Hermann are in Russia – a mysterious exhortation is concealed therein, a pain that leads into the open and permits both of them to share in the task assigned to me. (Heidegger 2008, 195/245)

Heidegger believed that his thinking as grown out of the "native soil" would have a "universal" relevance such that it could "incorporate 'the East'" (In my view, the "universal" here functions as a synonym of Beyng-historical). The "East" in relation to the "Evening Conversation" bears on the Russian East first and foremost but is not restricted to it. Heidegger extended this concern to the Asian East and perhaps to all of what could be called the "East" (probably for this reason he erased the names of Zhuangzi and Huizi in the "Evening Conversation"), although the "East" in his public writings often comes across as an abstract "East" without a clear designation. A good example is the phrase "the mysterious relations to the East" (*die geheimnisvollen Bezüge zum Osten*), which appears in the "Letter on Humanism" composed in 1946:

> But even the West [*Abendland*] is not thought regionally as the Occident in contrast to the Orient, nor merely as Europe, but rather world-historically out of nearness to the source. We have still scarcely begun to think of the mysterious relations to the East that found expression in Hölderlin's poetry. (Heidegger [1946], 257/338)

In the context of Heidegger's elucidations of Hölderlin's poetry, the "East" (and "Asia") refers predominantly to the Greek East. However, on some occasions Heidegger was juxtaposing the Russian *East* with the Greek *East*, and East *Asia* with Greek *Asia*. In doing so, he attempted to encompass everything under the umbrella of the first inception in the *Morgenland* versus the promising other inception of philosophy in the *Abendland*. Another passage from his writings of the same period shows this tendency.

> *We,* the poets; the word, that which destiny has sent us, that which is *to be said says,* that which unifies Asia and Europe, *Morgen-* and *Abendland,* while it "is" "over" them [*weil es «über » sie « ist »*], only [thus] supporting and enabling their hidden historical essence. (Heidegger [1945/46], 357–58)

The so-called unification of Asia – from which the Greek thinkers received the inspirations and creatively initiated the first inception – and Europe – into which the *Abendland* has submerged itself – makes sense only from out of the history of Beyng (since "the word" is Beyng). There are also such sayings as:

> Europe, considered in terms of continents, belongs to Asia [*Asien*].
> *Eurasia* – to it belongs Russia as well as Japan. (Heidegger [1941/42a], 80/95)

It sounds trivial to observe that, geographically speaking, what is called Europe is "no more than a geographical accident, the peninsula that Asia shoves into the Atlantic" (Sartre [1948], 292). If we take into account the interchange of the peoples living there, either by sea or by land, then we can sense that the subsequently divided continents and traditions are not a matter of given fact. It is curious that Heidegger listed Russia and Japan together as belonging to "Eurasia." Would that mean that for him the cultures of these two nations integrated the influences from both Europe and Asia? Among the countries in Asia, Japan was the first that implemented the policy of Westernization (since 1868). In articulating these geographical and cultural commonplaces, was Heidegger considering possible ways of connections between Europe and Asia both in antiquity and in modernity?

We can also ponder over the addition of the word "Asia" with an exclamation mark in Heidegger's letter to his brother on March 5, 1945, where he cited the passage on the necessity of the unneeded from the *Zhuangzi*: "The brief conversation between two Chinese thinkers (Asia! [*Asien*]) certainly gives you happiness" (Heidegger 2016, 123). Invoking the term of Asia discloses that Heidegger's concern exceeds the *specificity* of Zhuangzi's philosophy. Of course, it is the Greek East and/or Greek Asia that offers the final arbiter for making sense of Heidegger's efforts at ascribing a Beyng-historical significance to the Russian *East* and to East *Asia*.[59] Consequently, the question of whether and to what extent the Russian East and East Asia really live up to this Beyng-historical significance and could be able to maintain this status in Heidegger's juxtapositions defies a definitive answer.

6 A Different Configuration of the Confrontation/ Engagement with the Asiatic/Asia

As discussed in Section 3, Heidegger's thinking bearing on the Asiatic in the 1930s was fundamentally influenced by Nietzsche's radical distinction between the Dionysiac Greeks and the Dionysiac barbarians. However, we witness a metamorphosis of his conceptions when he revisited the theme of confrontation with the Asiatic in the 1960s. Heidegger's reflections were recorded in a slim book entitled *Sojourns* (*Aufenthalte*) (Heidegger [1962b]), which was later included in GA 75. It was composed on the basis of his first journey to Greece. In my view, Heidegger's new outlook on the Asiatic was inspired by Hölderlin's thinking regarding the nondialectical relations between the "Oriental," the Greeks, and the Germans. Heidegger begins *Sojourns* by citing

---

[59] Heidegger's efforts at ascribing a Beyng-historical significance to East Asia is most obvious in his 1953/54 "A Dialogue on Language" (cf. Ma 2008, chapters 8 & 9).

the fourth strophe of Hölderlin's poem "Bread and Wine," wherein the poet, to put it in Heidegger's words, "turned his gaze to the Greece that has already been" (Heidegger [1962b], 1/215). Hölderlin remained an implicit conversation partner throughout the whole text of *Sojourns*. Although Heidegger started to lecture on Hölderlin toward the mid-1930s, it took a long time for him to find a suitable way in which Hölderlin's ideas could be brought to bear on the Greeks' involvement with the Asiatic. Before engaging into an inquiry of Heidegger's new conceptions, I first review Hölderlin's relevant ideas.

Living in an age of what Schlegel called the "Oriental Renaissance," Hölderlin himself had a concern with Asian thought. When preparing his poetic novel *Hyperion*, he consulted Richard Chandler's *Travels in Asia Minor and Greece* (Oxford 1775/78) in German translation (Leipzig 1776/77) (cf. Görner 2021, 4). In his work, there appeared such terms as "the Oriental" (*das Morgenländische*), "Asia" (*Asien*), East (*Ost*), and "Egyptian." In his letters to his friend Böhlendorff, Hölderlin presented a pair of nondialectical relations between the "Oriental," the Greeks, and the Germans. Greek nature or ownness *(das Eigene)* is Oriental culture, that is, "the fire from heaven" or "the holy pathos"; this was achieved by successfully appropriating Oriental culture that was initially the foreign *(das Fremde)* to the Greeks, appropriating it by way of a "clarity of representation" and "Junonian sobriety" (these are Hölderlin's phrases cited by Heidegger) (cf. Heidegger [1934/35], 264/291). For instance, Hölderlin mentioned that Homer "was soulful enough to capture Western [*abendländische*], *Junonian sobriety* for his Apollonian kingdom, and thus to truly appropriate the foreign" (cited in Heidegger [1941/42b], 130/154). In citing this remark, Heidegger explains that Apollo is for Hölderlin "the name for what is light and fiery and glowing – the name for what Nietzsche thinks as the Dionysian and contrasts with the Apollonian" (Heidegger [1941/42b], 130/154).

German nature or ownness is Greek culture and art, that is, the "clarity of representation" and "Junonian sobriety," which could be called their endowment. Yet, it is urgent for the Germans to come up against that ownness as foreignness; alternatively speaking, the Germans should experience their nature (or ownness) (that is, the "clarity of representation" and "Junonian sobriety") as Oriental, that is, as "the fire from heaven" or "the holy pathos." This is the historical task that befalls the Germans.[60] However, here arises a problematic that Warminski suggested. Because the "Oriental" or "Egyptian" is in the final analysis the foreign for the Greeks and not for the Germans, when the Greek nature is represented as the "Oriental" or as the "Egyptian," the otherness (that is, the "Oriental" or "Egyptian") of the Greeks is suppressed. Alternatively

---

[60] Compare Warminski's illuminating discussions (Warminski 1987, 35, 54–55, 68).

speaking, when the Germans invent their Greeks, the "Oriental" or "Egyptian" gets disarticulated or becomes asymmetricalized (cf. Warminski, 1987, 55). This also implies that the true Oriental could only be accessed via the mediation by the Greeks.

From Heidegger's perspective, the later evolvement of metaphysics displays a unilateral emphasis on clarity and sobriety to the neglect of "fire" and "pathos." He called this lineage of post-Hellenic metaphysics "Occidental" and radically distinguished it from Western (*abendländische*) philosophy that enjoyed a unique bond with the Greek inception as the "Oriental" (*das Morgenländische*) or Asia (cf. Heidegger [1941/42a], 83/99). To put it in his own words, "For Hölderlin, Greece is the Other of the Western [*abendländische*] world. The one and the other belong within a singular history" (Heidegger [1934/35], 70/78). Labeling Greece as "the Oriental" (*das Morgenländische*) highlights its intertwinement with the Evening-land (*Abendland*) as distinguished from the corrupted "Occidental." Giving Greece the epithet of "Asia" keeps it at a remove from contemporary Europe that has become planetary and into which the *Abendland* has submerged itself. When Greece is considered as the proper other of the *Abendland*, it becomes a pressing task to excavate and revitalize its modes of mindfulness that are foreign to the Occidental ways of inquiry. In the meantime, however, there is the worry that the original Oriental or the Asiatic has been completely forgotten, or at most could only serve as a detour for recovering what I call the Beyng-historical significance of the Greek East. As Heidegger puts it in *Ponderings*:

> To be sure, Hölderlin does not poetically enter serene climes – *nor does he take refuge in the oases of the desert* – but he does venture newly, differently, and solely into the "primeval confusion" [*uralte Verwirrung*] – and the latter is what we must think in advance as the abyss of the fullness of essential decisions [*den Abgrund der wesentlichen Entscheidungsfülle*]. (Heidegger [1939–1941], 12–13/15; emphasis added)

Heidegger assumed that Hölderlin had no more intention than he did to dwell in the (supposedly Egyptian) oases of the desert. Hölderlin's originality lies in a renewed articulation and expression of the forgotten "primeval confusion," and Heidegger associated it with his own notions of abyss and of decision. *Entscheidung*, the German word for "decision," contains the word *Scheidung*, which means "separation." In using this word, Heidegger was entertaining the idea of the ontological difference of Beyng and being. The idea that Beyng cannot be reduced to a particular being fits with the image of Beyng as "primeval confusion" that embraces all. This neglected sense of Beyng resonates with the implications of the Being-historical Asiatic.

Hölderlin was as much an admirer of the Greek world as Nietzsche was. However, he has never intimated any idea like a "vast gulf which separated the *Dionysiac Greeks* from the Dionysiac barbarians" (Nietzsche [1872], 20/31). Although possible problematics as discussed in the foregoing may arise in Heidegger's appropriation of Hölderlin's ideas concerning the relations between the "Oriental," the Greeks, and the Germans, I suggest that when in the 1960s Heidegger reconsidered the "confrontation" with the Asiatic – on one occasion he used the word "Asia" in quotation marks (cf. Heidegger [1962b], 25/228) – such problematics abated but were not completely dissolved. If we call Heidegger's comportment toward the (alien) Asiatic in the 1930s a Nietzschean oppositional model, then his comportment toward the Asiatic/ Asia in the 1960s exhibited a Hölderlinean nondialectical model (This does not mean that Heidegger has abandoned all of Nietzsche's ideas). In the latter context, the word *Auseinandersetzung* can be translated as "engagement."

In the early part of *Sojourns*, Heidegger urged the necessity of a "mindful retrospect [*sinnenden Rückblickes*]" on what "ancient remembrance [*uralt Gedächtnis*] has preserved for us and what remains distorted" (Heidegger [1962b], 3/216). This is preceded by a reminder that the current human world as dominated by machination (*Machenschaften*) was bordering on self-destruction and annihilation. It is a world in which the gods have taken flight and the dwelling place of human beings has become desolate (Heidegger [1962b], 1/215). Heidegger rehearsed his idea concerning the later distortions of Hellenic philosophy, but now putting an emphasis on the domination of modern science and technology, to which such distortions ultimately led. In deciding to take a journey to Greece, Heidegger expected to experience the "originary Greekness [*anfänglich Griechischen*]," and he mentioned as a contrast the story that Wolfgang Goethe allegedly sensed "the nearness of Greekness" in Sicily, but he interpreted that as a Roman-Italian Greece (Heidegger [1962b], 8/219).[61] Meanwhile, Heidegger referred to his first encounter with Greece via reading Homer and studying Greek sculpture in the Gymnasium, though their Greekness only came to dawn on him in his later studies and in his engagement (*Auseinandersetzung*) with ancient (Greek) thinking (Heidegger [1962b], 11/220; 18/224).

During the journey, Heidegger twice mentioned the pre-Hellenic world. The first time was in Mycenae, where Heidegger felt a "resistance [*Abwehr*]" against this pre-Hellenic world, though he said it was "the critical exchange

---

[61] As a Romanticist, Goethe had an interest in the East. He has proposed the cosmopolitan "world literature" (*Weltliteratur*) paradigm, and he drew on the Persian poet Hafiz in composing his famous *West-East Divan* (1819). When studying at the Gymnasium, Heidegger was well read in German literature, including Goethe.

[*Auseinandersetzung*] that first *helped* the Greeks achieve their ownness" (Heidegger [1962b], 19/224; emphasis added). Notably, Heidegger was speaking of their relation in terms of "help." The second time was in Knossos, a town on the island of Crete, where a feminine divinity assumed the center place, and an "Egyptian-Oriental essence [*Ägyptisch-orientalisches Wesen*]" came into view (Heidegger [1962b], 23/227). Heidegger doubted that the archaeological objects as displayed in the museum were only their gleaming surfaces and hence could not conceal anything. On this occasion he was more dubious about the "essence" of the Oriental world.

When the ship reached the Island of Rhodes, a host of considerations occupied Heidegger.

> We had approached the coast of Asia Minor. Are we farther away from Greekness [*Griechischen*]? Or are we already within the domain of its destiny [*Geschick*], which was structured [*fügte*] through its confrontation with "Asia" [*Asia*] by transforming the wild and appeasing [*versöhnte*] the passion [*Leidenschaft*] with something "greater" [*ein Größeres*], which remained great for the mortals and so it granted them the place for reverend awe? (Heidegger [1962b], 25/228)

As mentioned earlier, the word "Asiatic" is now taken to be offensive because of its association with the history of colonialism. Hence, it is perplexing why in these questionings, instead of "Asiatic," Heidegger used the word "Asia," setting it into citation marks and yet related it to "the wild" and "the passion." Think of his remarks on "the unbridled, the unrestrained, the ecstatic and wild, the raving, the Asiatic" when referring to Nietzsche's distinction of the Apollonian and the Dionysian (Heidegger [1933/34], 74/92). For Nietzsche, the wildness and the passions as exhibited at the festivals for both the Greeks and the Asians remained the same, but they were infused with different significations. Could it be the case here that Heidegger was considering a conflation of the Being-historical Asiatic with the Asiatic that was overcome by the Greeks because they assume the same destructive ontological power that has determined the destiny of the West? This does not mean that the two different meanings of the Asiatic (as discussed in Section 3) now collapse into the same, but rather that Heidegger in the 1930s did not yet think through the internal link between the two and thus conveyed them as two completely different terms. In fact, both kinds of Asiatic lie at the ground of the ontological power that is indispensable for the self-transformation of Western philosophical tradition. In the following passage, Heidegger retrieved the term "Asiatic":

> [T]he confrontation with the Asiatic [*Asiatischen*] was for the Greek Dasein a fruitful necessity [*fruchtbare Notwendigkeit*]. This confrontation is for us

today – in an entirely different way and to a far greater extent – the decision about the destiny [*Schicksal*] of Europe and what calls itself the West-oriented world [*westliche Welt*]. (Heidegger [1962b], 25/228)

In reconsidering the confrontation with the Asiatic, Heidegger no longer employed the negative terms regarding the Asiatic that he used in the 1930s and only spoke of it as "a fruitful necessity." The word "fruitful" reminds us of his remark in terms of "a fruitful confrontation/engagement with East Asian 'thinking' [*eine fruchtbare Auseinandersetzung mit dem ostasiatischen 'Denken'*]," where he said that "[s]uch a confrontation/engagement could help [*mithelfen*] with the task of saving the essential nature of human being from the threat of an extreme technological calculation and manipulation of human Dasein" (Heidegger [1968], 695). It is not improbable that due to his sustained contact with East Asian thinkers and due to his increasing worry about the *Gestell*, Heidegger softened his earlier harsh attitude toward the Asiatic that was allegedly "overcome" by the Greeks.

A concern with the technological world pervaded the whole text of *Sojourns*. In the cited passage, Heidegger's juxtaposition of Europe and "what calls itself the West-oriented world" (he did not use the word *Abendland* that has Being-historical significance) reminds us of his idea that currently *Abendland* is submerged into Europe, and that "'Europe' is the actualization of the *decline* [*Untergang*] *of the West* [*Abendland*]" (Heidegger [1939–41], 217/273; cf. Ma 2021). The West-oriented world here refers to the Anglo-American world that stemmed from the completion of metaphysics. Following this paragraph, Heidegger turned to the contemporary world situation where modern technology dominates the globe with the impending threat of atomic powers. The urgency of acquiring a free relation to Beyng that is "capable of warding off the violence in the essence of technology" makes it timely to reflect on the ownness (*das Eigene*) of Greece, especially in relation to its decisive confrontation with the Asiatic (Heidegger [1962b], 26/228). At this point, Heidegger resumed the topic on the Asiatic:

As the blue of the sky and the sea changed by the hour, the thought arose, whether the Orient [*Orient*] could be for us still a rising [*Aufgang*] of light and clarity [*Erleuchtung*], or rather whether these are only illusionary lights that feign the revelation to come from there and thus are nothing more than historical fabrications artificially sustained.

The Asiatic once brought to the Greeks a dark fire, whose flames their poetizing and thinking formed [*fügten*] into brightness [*Helle*] and measure. In this way, Heraclitus had to think the All [*All*] of things present as κόσμος. (Heidegger [1962b], 26–27/ 229)

The association of the Orient with light reminds us of the phrase *ex oriente lux*. It was widely recognized that Heraclitus' thought had a special bond with Zoroasterism that worshipped light. Heidegger obviously refrained from using strong locutions such as "the greatest opposite" and "the most alien and most difficult" in relation to the Orient. Rather, he presented his pondering in a series of mild questionings. Following the association of the Orient with light and uttering his ambivalence regarding the contributions of the Orient, Heidegger characterized the Asiatic as a "dark fire" which the Greeks tamed into "brightness and measure."

We must keep in mind that the word "dark" is nothing negative for Heidegger. Some pages later, he spoke of "the darkness [*Dunkel*] of destiny" in which all the light of Greek Dasein hid itself (Heidegger [1962b], 49/241). In Section 4, we come across him speaking of "a genuine darkness" with respect to Russianism (Heidegger [1938/39a], 314/402). In *Sojourns*, Heidegger was not speaking of the Asiatic as "the mythical in general" any more but said that it brought "a dark fire" to the Greeks. Under its influence, Heraclitus developed his idea of κόσμος, which Heidegger interpreted as "the lighting" and as "the fire that keeps rising" (Heidegger [1962b], 27–28/229).

In Heidegger's earlier work, he almost never seriously considered the hinges on which the Asiatic was related to Heraclitus. In the 1934/1935 lecture course, he only spoke of Heraclitus as the name of "of a primordial power of Western-Germanic historical Dasein" whereas the Asiatic was not examined on its own terms (Heidegger [1934/35], 118/134). In *Sojourns*, he approached their connection via their shared theme of "fire." Almost two millennia ago, the theologian Clement of Alexandria (circa 115–215) commented that Heraclitus' doctrine of purification by fire came from "barbarian philosophy" (cf. West 1971, 165). Friedrich Creuzer (1771–1858) – a contemporary of Hölderlin – thus described this connection:

> Heraclitus thought and taught in the spirit of Zoroaster, only penetrating what he had taken from the East with the shafts of clear Hellenic logic and reducing it to a coherent system so as to make it acceptable to his people. (Cited in West 1971, 166)[62]

This formulation of Heraclitus' relation to the East is dialectical, but we know that Heraclitus himself did not construct "a coherent system." Such a "system" resulted from modern conceptions that worshipped coherence. Heidegger would be opposed to such a dialectical view. The "fire" and the "passion" in Heidegger's text echo Hölderlin's phrases of "the fire from heaven" and "the

---

[62] For a detailed account of Heraclitus' connection with Persian religion, compare West 1971, 165–202.

holy pathos," which constituted the Greek ownness that is appropriated from Oriental culture by means of "clarity of representation" and "Junonian sobriety" (cited in Heidegger [1934/35], 264/291). Hölderlin's ideas parallel Heidegger's observation here that the flames of the dark fire from the Asiatic were formed into brightness and measure by the Greeks' poetizing and thinking.

Moreover, if the word "dark" echoes Nietzsche's characterization of the Dionysian and the word "measure" corresponds to Nietzsche's description of the Apollonian. Just as the Greek Apollonianism grew out of a Dionysian underground, the Heraclitan fire received its kindling from the Asiatic dark fire. In both passages in which "fire" and "passion" appear in Heidegger's text, the Asiatic assumed the role of protagonist. It was neither denied nor suppressed, as may be the case in Heidegger's writings in the 1930s. Hence, Heidegger's pondering on the confrontation/engagement with the Asiatic in *Sojourns* assumed a configuration different from that in the 1930s, a configuration that can be called a Hölderlinean nondialectical model. It is nondialectical insofar as for Heidegger fire and passion were not extinguished by being absorbed into a purely intellectual system. Instead, fire and passion remained and called for being rekindled and rethought. Of course, this relation was tarnished by an asymmetry inasmuch as the relation was considered unilaterally from the Greek side alone to the neglect of the other side, that is, the intellectual unfolding of Asian traditions in their own right.[63]

In a note written between 1943–45 and published in GA 73.1, Heidegger refers to Brahma from the Indian tradition in relation to the Greeks and "fire," and he also mentions Dionysus:

> *The Greeks and Brahma.*
> The Greeks have not eliminated [*beseitigt*] the fire – but given it a form [*gestaltet*].
> (Dionysus – hearth [*Estia*] – Empedocles! Hell – fire – light – not reach light – brightness – *semblance* [*Schein*] – *spectacle* [*Anblick*] – doxa.)
> (Heidegger 2013, 230)

This is a rare case where Heidegger named a Hindu god from the Indian tradition. The thoughts articulated here broadly conform to our preceding analyses. The phrase "*semblance*" reminds us of his remark in *Sojourns* concerning whether the Orient was still "a rising of light and clarity" or it only gave illusionary lights and amounted to "historical fabrications artificially sustained" (Heidegger [1962b], 26/ 229). This means that Heidegger suspected that, under the sway of modernity and planetarization, what today was presented as the

---

[63] This asymmetry resembles that found in Heidegger's 1953/54 essay "A Dialogue on Language" (cf. Ma 2008, chapter 8).

Orient had lost its ownness and retained only a façade of the Oriental. This makes it more relevant to keep away from current fabrications and to retrieve the essence of the Orient in its first encounter with the Greeks (of course, from Heidegger's perspective, the latter is more of a task for the thinkers from the East).

Heidegger resumed his journey of searching for Greekness. He claimed that it was on the island of Delos – the birthplace of Apollo and his sister Artemis (who was at home in the shelter of wilderness) – that he discovered the ownness of the Greeks because the island itself was "that region [*Bereich*] of the unconcealed hiddenness, which accords sojourn" (Heidegger [1962b], 34/233). This interdependence of the unconcealed and the concealed is named Ἀλήθεια, and "Heraclitus' word of κόσμος as πῦρ [fire] becomes meaningful only from the name of Ἀλήθεια as Ἑστία [hearth]" (Heidegger [1962b], 33/233).[64] With Ἀλήθεια, Heidegger's most favorite word for truth, Greek thinking reached a sort of apex. After reaching this point, Heidegger did not forget to mention the tension between the Greek people and the "barbarous":

> Despite their desire [*Lust*] for navigation, the citizens and ethnic groups [*Seine Menschen und Volkschaften*] [of Greece] knew settledness [*Seßhaftigkeit*] and the border against the barbarous [*Barbarische*] in favor of the seat of the gods. (Heidegger [1962b], 43–44/238)

After presenting a Hölderlinean nondialectical model concerning the confrontation/engagement with the Asiatic/Asia, Heidegger turned around to stress the sought-for uniqueness of the Greekness, for the sake of which he set upon the journey. At the same time, he was reminded of the border – which was in fact not unsurpassable – between the Greeks and the barbarous. Did Nietzsche's distinction of the Dionysiac Greeks and the Dionysiac barbarians occur to Heidegger once again?

Conclusion

Heidegger's contemporary Karl Jaspers coined the notion of "Axial Age," which placed on the same plane a plurality of civilizations flourishing between 800 and 200 BCE. Unlike Jaspers who was more forthcoming about learning from non-Western philosophers, Heidegger's thinking with regard to Eastern/Asian thought is much more deeply concealed and thus requires much more effort to excavate.[65] This task becomes more demanding in view of the manifoldness of his thinking and its metamorphosis in different phases. As

---

[64] Heidegger's original text used the capitalized forms of these two Greek words.

[65] For "Axial Age," compare Jaspers 1949. Heidegger has criticized the notion of "Axial Age" (cf. Ma 2008, 63–65).

Heidegger himself said of his *Denkweg*: "The indicated path, in retrospect and in prospect, appears with every sojourn [*Aufenthalt*] in a different light, with a different tone, and stirs different interpretations [*Deutungen*]" (Heidegger [1957], 10/55).

Heidegger devoted his entire life to discovering suitable ways of making humans prepared for listening to the call of Being/Beyng, and on many occasions he has insisted on a "simple saying" (*einfache Sagen*), which denotes something resembling a soliloquy of Beyng itself (Heidegger 2008, 182/228). The character of multiplicity inherent to his single path of thinking on Being/Beyng has made it open, nevertheless, to a multiplicity of interpretations, including an Orientalization of his ideas, of which Heidegger himself was aware –especially in relation to his Japanese reception – and about which he remained ambivalent. I suggest that we can gain a vantage point to understand the intricacies of Heidegger's comportment toward the East/Asia from the perspective of his turn from the guiding question of "Being" (*Sein*) to the abyssal question of "Beyng" (*Seyn*) with an eye to his consequent attempt at a conflation of both terms.[66]

Heidegger started to use *Seyn* extensively in his 1934/35 lecture course on Hölderlin. In the *Contributions to Philosophy* of 1936–38, he explained that using *Seyn* "is supposed to indicate that *Sein* is here no longer being thought metaphysically" (Heidegger [1936–38], 344/436). In his *Ponderings* and in most of his nonpublic writings on the history of Beyng composed during 1936–42, Heidegger has almost always used *Seyn*. For Heidegger, traditional metaphysics belongs to the Occidental – with Being as the guiding question – while the nonmetaphysical Beyng-historical thinking belongs to the Western (*abendländisch*) – with Beyng as the abyssal question and with Greece – the Morning-land – as the place of the first inception.

During his *Sein* phase before the mid-1930s, Heidegger exhibited a comportment toward Eastern traditions and alien cultures that was dominated by resistance and opposition. The case with *Being and Time* is more compli-cated. In Division Two, Heidegger assumed an attitude of dismissal regarding the significance of Eastern influences for the sake of reinvigorating Dasein's true historicality whereas in Division One he was more open toward the possibility that Dasein's existential-ontological structure is not fixed and invari-able but could be modified (if not completely overhauled) on the basis of the alternative existentiell input rendered from analyses of primitive Dasein or of mythical Dasein.

Heidegger's pondering on the early Greeks' involvement with the Asiatic in the 1930s is in general characterized by a Nietzschean oppositional model. His

---

[66] Compare Ma 2019 for an explanation of "the abyssal question."

notion of what I call the Beyng-historical (Greek) Asiatic, nevertheless, shows a sign of moving toward nonmetaphysical Beyng. Against traditional metaphysics, which he regarded as belonging to the Occidental, Heidegger depicted the primordial ontological powers – to be understood in the Greek sense – as "the unbridled, the unrestrained, the ecstatic and wild, the raving, the Asiatic" (Heidegger [1933/34], 74/92). In this connection he juxtaposed Greece (the Morning-land) with the East, Asia, Asia Minor, and so on. We can discern that a possibility for a transition of Heidegger's comportment toward the East is hidden in his notion of the Beyng-historical Asiatic. Nonetheless, at this stage he continued to be enthralled by Nietzsche's radical differentiation between the Dionysiac Greeks and the Dionysiac barbarians and hardly probed into the internal connection between the Greek Asiatic and the alien Asiatic.

With respect to his *Seyn* phase that began in the mid-1930s and remained active till the mid-1940s, I have discussed Heidegger's ponderings on Russianism and his appropriation of the *Zhuangzi*. We find that Heidegger took most seriously the possibility that the Russian East, which had inherited the original notion of spirit as σοφία in the form of mysticism, could bring about recuperation of the world that has been abandoned by Beyng. The Beyng-historical weight Heidegger ascribed to Russianism was integrally bound up with the project of twisting free of past metaphysics that has almost completely lost its mystic and spiritual tradition. We also see that Heidegger's discussion of "the necessity of the unneeded" in the "Evening Conversation" – drawing on a passage from chapter 26 of the *Zhuangzi* concerning the usefulness of the useless – corresponds very well to his configuration of Beyng in terms of the unneeded (*Un-nötige*) or the ne-cessary (*Not-wendige*) in his writings of the late 1930s and early 1940s.

After the end of World War II, it seems that the hope Heidegger placed upon Russianism could not be substantiated – at least not in the short term. Should he openly discuss those ideas that he has carefully kept secret in his nonpublic writings, he might well come under pressure. Probably because of these concerns, Heidegger had never disclosed to the public his relevant thoughts on Russianism during his lifetime. The following remark made in the 1966 *Der Spiegel*'s interview can be regarded as an exception, but that interview only came to light a few days after Heidegger's death on May 26, 1976:

> [W]ho of us can decide whether or not one day in Russia and China the venerable traditions [*uralte Überlieferungen*] of a 'thinking' will awaken which will help make possible for humanity a free relationship to the technological world? (Heidegger [1966], 281/677)

With the aid of our study of Heidegger's reflection on Russianism, we are finally able to appreciate the weight he accorded to Russia. The mention of Russia in the interview did not just come out of the blue. With Heidegger becoming reticent about Russianism, he turned his eyes to the world of East Asia, especially in relation to East Asian languages. In a letter to his wife dated October 16, 1955, he wrote:[67]

> The problem of language has been ramifying constantly since I've begun to have some idea of the structure of East Asian languages. I don't want to say anything premature in the talk here.[68] (Heidegger 2008, 250/309)

This remark aptly exemplifies Heidegger's often ambivalent attitude. Whenever Heidegger directly spoke of a dialogue with the East Asian world in the 1950s and 1960s, he always referred to "a dialogue [*Gespräch*] with the Greek thinkers and their language" as the precondition of the former dialogue (Heidegger [1953], 157/41; cf. Ma 2008, chapter 3). How to make sense of this idiosyncratic Beyng-historical order? A possible answer to this question is two-folded. On the one hand, Heidegger insisted that Western thinking must first accomplish self-transformation from its own root – the Greek inception – without Eastern intervention. On the other hand, according to Heidegger, currently all the corners of the planet were under the sway of European thinking, that is, metaphysics. As he wrote in a volume belonging to the *Black Notebooks*, "All modern – also all of the East [*das des Ostens*] – belongs to metaphysics" (Heidegger [2015], 112).[69] The Eastern world should overcome such Europeanization by its own initiative and retrieve its own "venerable inceptions [*ehrwürdigen Anfänge*]" before it could engage in a genuine East–West dialogue (Heidegger [1953/54], 37,124).

In the foregoing, I have reviewed Heidegger's comportment to the East/Asia in relation to his *Sein* phase and his *Seyn* phase. Although Heidegger distinguished between Being and Beyng in terms of metaphysical and nonmetaphysical, in the early 1940s he envisioned a nondual relation between them. For instance, he said, "Beyng overcomes the dominance of the distorted essence not by 'engaging' [*abgibt*] with it and overpowering it but, rather, by letting the distorted essence go into its demise" (Heidegger [1941/42a], 70–71/84). In this sense, Heidegger speaks of the futuristic to-be-re-initiated *abendländischen* metaphysics as "the same metaphysics" that is to be overcome (he was not

---

[67] For Heidegger's various inquiries about Asian languages, compare Ma 2008, chapter 7.

[68] "The talk" probably refers to the well-known lecture entitled "Gelassenheit," which Heidegger delivered in Messkirch on October 30, 1955 (Heidegger [1955a]).

[69] The exact year in which Heidegger wrote this note was unknown. It came from GA 97, *Anmerkungen I-V*, all the notes were written during 1942 to 1948.

strict with the usage of "metaphysics" either) (cf. Heidegger [1941/42], 83/99). This explains why Heidegger in most of his public writings since the mid-1940s did not keep to a consistent differentiation of Being and Beyng.[70]

Suppose we call Heidegger's *Sein* phase the Occidental line and his *Seyn* phase the Oriental line, and since the *Morgenland* – as indissolubly bound up with all kinds of East – is indispensable for the *Abendland*, then we can discern the ways in which Heidegger opened the promise of a dialogue with the East and yet stepped back from that threshold. The word "East," or "Asia," indicates a nexus in which all the possible designations could find a place, though it often remains unclear how much weight Heidegger apportions to each possible designation. The Occidental line, whose real foundation lies in the Roman imperial culture – the Greek inception was only retrospectively acknowledged through the Roman mediation – was more exclusive with respect to Eastern traditions whereas the Oriental line takes into account contributions by non-Greek traditions to the flourishment of philosophy in Greece (even when Heidegger relied on a problematic Nietzschean model concerning such a confrontation) and it offers the potential for reconsidering the relation to the East/Asia. This sort of potential is exemplified by Heidegger's reconfiguration of the early Greeks' confrontation/engagement with the Asiatic/Asia.

However, along with Heidegger's conflation of *Sein* and *Seyn* after World War II, he came to understate the difference that he made between the *abendländisch* and the *Westlich* and instead stresses the unique bond of the *Abendland* and Europe. Thus, in the lecture "What Is Philosophy?" he declared:

> "The statement – philosophy is in its essence Greek – says nothing more than: The West [*Abendland*] and Europe, and only these, are in the innermost course of their history originarily 'philosophical.'" (Heidegger [1955b], 31/30).

Heidegger's vacillation between the Occidental line and the Oriental line tells us that an East–West perspective is indispensable not only for an adequate understanding and evaluation of his thinking but also for a more enriched reconfiguration of philosophy in the current and the future age.

---

[70] For more explications concerning the nondual relation between *abendländische* philosophy and Occidental philosophy, compare Ma 2023.

References

Adluri, Vishwa, & Joydeep Bagchee. 2014. *The Nay Science: A History of German Indology*. Oxford: Oxford University Press.

Bambach, Charles. 2003. *Heidegger's Roots: Nietzsche, National Socialism, and the Greeks*. Ithaca, NY: Cornell University Press.

Bernasconi, Robert. 1995. On Heidegger's Other Sins of Omission. *American Catholic Philosophical Quarterly* 69(2), 333–50.

Bilimoria, Purushottama. 2008. Nietzsche as "Europe's Buddha" and "Asia's Superman." *Sophia* 47(3): 359–76.

Brecht, Bertolt. 1989. Der gute Mensch von Sezuan. In *Werke*. Frankfurt: Suhrkamp. Band 6. 177–281.

Buber, Martin. [1910]. Zhuangzi: Sayings and Parables. In *Chinese Tales*. New Jersey: Humanities Press International, Inc. (1991), 1–107. *Reden und Gleichnisse des Tschuang-tse*. In *Werkausgabe*. Band 2.3. *Schriften zur chinesischen Philosophie und Literatur*. Gütersloh: Gütersloher Verlagshaus (2013), 51–130.

Camilleri, Sylvain & Daniel Proulx. 2014. Martin Heidegger et Henry Corbin: Lettres et documents (1930–1941). *Bulletin heideggérien* 4, 4–63.

Caputo, John D. 1978. *The Mystical Element in Heidegger's Thought*. Athens: Ohio University Press.

Corbin, Henry. 1993. *History of Islamic Philosophy*. Translated by Liadain Sherrard. London: Kegan Paul International.

Dostoevsky, Fyodor M. 1919. *The Diary of a Writer*. Translated and annotated by Boris Brasol. New York: Charles Scribner's Sons.

Druart, Thérèse-Anne. 1988. *Arabic Philosophy and the West: Continuity and Interaction*. Washington, DC: Georgetown University Press.

Elman, Benjamin A. 1983. Nietzsche and Buddhism. *Journal of the History of Ideas* 44(4), 671–86.

El-Bizri, Nader. 2000. *The Phenomenological Quest: Between Avicenna and Heidegger*. Binghamton, NY: Global Publications.

Farin, Ingo. 2016. Count Paul Yorck von Wartenburg. *The Stanford Encyclopedia of Philosophy*. Ed. Edward N. Zalta. https://plato.stanford.edu/archives/fall2016/entries/yorck/.

Figes, Orlando. 2003. *Natasha's Dance: A Cultural History of Russia*. New York: Picador.

Giles, Herbert Allen. 1889. *Chuang Tzu, Mystic, Moralist and Social Reformer*. London: Bernard Quaritch.

Görner, Rüdiger. 2021. *Hölderlin and the Consequences: An Essay on the German "Poet of Poets."* London: Palgrave Macmillan.

Grove, Philip B., Ed. 1966. *Webster's Third New International Dictionary of the English Language Unabridged.* Springfield, MA: G. C. Merriam Company.

Heidegger, Martin. [1910]. *Per mortem ad vitam*: Thoughts on Johannes Jörgensen's *Lies of Life and Truth of Life.* In *Supplements: From the Earliest Essays to Being and Time and Beyond.* Ed. John van Buren. New York: State University of New York Press (2002), 35–38. Per mortem ad vitam (Gedanken über *Jörgensens* »Lebenslüge und Lebenswahrheit«). In GA 16, *Reden und andere Zeugnisse eines Lebensweges 1910–1976* (2000), 3–6.

[1915a]. The War-Triduum in Messkirch. In *Becoming Heidegger: On the Trail of His Early Occasional Writing 1910–1927.* Ed. Theodore Kisiel & Thomas Sheehan. 2nd revised and expanded ed. Seattle: Noesis Press (2010), 51–54.

[1915b]. The Concept of Time in the Science of History. In *Becoming Heidegger.* Ed. Theodore Kisiel & Thomas Sheehan. Seattle: Noesis Press (2010), 63–76. Der Zeitbegriff in der Geschichtswissenschaft. In *GA 1, Frühe Schriften* (1978), 415–33.

[1915c]. Die Kategorien- und Bedeutungslehre des Duns Scotus. In GA 1, *Frühe Schriften* (1978), 189–411.

[1919a]. The Idea of Philosophy and the Problem of Worldview. War Emergency Semester 1919. In *Towards the Definition of Philosophy.* London: The Athlone Press (2000), 1–99. Die Idee der Philosophie und das Weltanschauungsproblem. In GA 56–57, *Zur Bestimmung der Philosophie* (1987), 1–117.

[1919b]. Phenomenology and Transcendental Philosophy of Value. Summer Semester 1919. In *Towards the Definition of Philosophy.* London: The Athlone Press (2000), 101–71. Phänomenologie und Transzendentale Wertphilosophie. In GA 56–57, *Zur Bestimmung der Philosophie* (1987), 119–203.

[1920/21]. *The Phenomenology of Religious Life.* Translated by Matthias Fritsch and Jennifer Anna Gosetti-Ferencei. Bloomington: Indiana University Press (2004). GA 60, *Phänomenologie des Religiösen Lebens* (1995).

[1923/24]. *Introduction to Phenomenological Research.* Bloomington: Indiana University Press (2005). GA 17, *Einführung in die phänomenologische Forschung* (1994).

[1924]. *Plato's Sophist.* Bloomington: Indiana University Press (1997). GA 19, *Platon: Sophistes* (1992).

[1925]. Wilhelm Dilthey's Research and the Current Struggle for a Historical Worldview. In *Becoming Heidegger*. Eds. Theodore Kisiel & Thomas Sheehan. Seattle: Noesis Press (2010), 238–40. Wilhelm Diltheys Forschungsarbeit und der gegenwärtige Kampf um eine historische Weltanschauung (April 1925). In GA 16, *Reden und andere Zeugnisse eines Lebensweges 1910–1976* (2000), 49–51.

[1926a]. On the Essence of Truth (lecture on Pentecost Monday 1926). In *Becoming Heidegger*. Eds. Theodore Kisiel & Thomas Sheehan. Seattle: Noesis Press (2010), 274–87.

[1926b]. *Basic Concepts of Ancient Philosophy.* Bloomington: Indiana University Press (2008). GA 22, *Die Grundbegriffe der Antiken Philosophie* (1993).

[1926/27]. GA 23, *Geschichte der Philosophie von Thomas von Aquin bis Kant* (2006).

[1927a]. *Being and Time.* Translated by J. Macquarrie and E. Robinson. San Francisco: Harper (1962). *Sein und Zeit*. Tübingen: Niemeyer (2002).

[1927b]. *The Basic Problems of Phenomenology.* Revised ed. Bloomington: Indiana University Press (1982). GA 24, *Die Grundprobleme der Phänomenologie* (1975).

[1928a]. Review of Ernst Cassirer: Philosophy of Symbolic Forms. Part Two: Mythical Thought. Berlin, 1925. In *Kant and the Problem of Metaphysics*. 5th ed. Bloomington: Indiana University Press (1997), 180–90. Ernst Cassirer, Philosophie der symbolischen Formen. 2. Teil: Das mythische Denken. Berlin 1925. In GA 3, *Kant und das Problem der Metaphysik* (1991), 255–70.

[1928b]. *The Metaphysical Foundations of Logic.* Bloomington: Indiana University Press (1984). GA 26, *Metaphysische Anfangsgründe der Logik im Ausgang von Leibniz* (1978).

[1928/29]. GA 27, *Einleitung in die Philosophie* (1990).

[1929/1930]. *The Fundamental Concepts of Metaphysics: World, Finitude, Solitude.* Bloomington: Indiana University Press (1995). GA 29/30, *Die Grundbegriffe der Metaphysik: Welt, Endlichkeit, Einsamkeit* (1983).

[1930]. Vom Wesen der Wahrheit. Vortrag am 8. Oktober 1930 in Bremen. In GA 80.1, *Vorträge* (Teil 1: 1915 bis 1932) (2016), 345–77.

[1932]. *The Beginnings of Western Philosophy: Interpretations of Anaximander and Parmenides.* Bloomington: Indiana University Press (2015). GA 35, *Der Anfang der abendländischen Philosophie: Auslegung of Anaximander und Parmenides* (2012).

[1933/34]. On the Essence of Truth. In *Being and Truth*. Bloomington: Indiana University Press (2010), 67–201. Vom Wesen der Wahrheit. In GA 36/37, *Sein und Wahrheit* (2001), 83–264.

[1934]. Die Gegenwärtige Lage und die künftige Aufgabe der deutschen Philosophie. In GA 16, *Reden und andere Zeugnisse eines Lebensweges 1910–1976* (2000), 316–34.

[1934/35]. *Hölderlin's Hymns "Germania" and "The Rhine."* Bloomington: Indiana University Press (2014). GA 39, *Hölderlins Hymnen "Germanien" und "der Rhein"* (1980).

[1935]. *Introduction to Metaphysics.* New Haven, CT: Yale University Press (2000). *Einführung in die Metaphysik.* Tübingen: Max Niemeyer Verlag (1998).

[1936a]. *Schelling's Treatise on the Essence of Human Freedom.* Athens: Ohio University Press (1985). GA 42, *Schelling: Vom Wesen der menschlichen Freiheit* (1988).

[1936b]. Europa und die deutsche Philosophie (April 8, 1936). In GA 80.2 *Vorträge* (Teil 2: 1935–1967) (2020), 679–96.

[1936–38]. *Contributions to Philosophy (Of the Event).* Bloomington: Indiana University Press (2012). GA 65, *Beiträge zur Philosophie (Vom Ereignis)* (1989).

[1937]. Wege zur Aussprache. In GA 13, *Aus der Erfahrung des Denken 1910–1976* (1983), 15–21.

[1937/38]. *Basic Questions of Philosophy.* Bloomington: Indiana University Press (1994). GA 45, *Grundfragen der Philosophie* (1984).

1938. *Qu'est-ce que la métaphysique? Suivi d'extraits sur l'être et le temps et d'une conférence sur Hölderlin.* Trans. Henry Corbin. Paris: Gallimard.

[1938/39a]. *Ponderings VII–XI: Black Notebooks 1938–1939.* Bloomington: Indiana University Press (2017). GA 95, *Überlegungen VII–XI (Schwarze Hefte 1938/39)* (2014).

[1938/39b]. Metaphysik und Nihilismus. In GA 67, *Die Überwindung der Metaphysik* (1999), 1–174

[1938–40]. *The History of Beyng.* Bloomington: Indiana University Press (2015). GA 69, *Die Geschichte des Seyns* (1998).

[1939–41]. *Ponderings XII–XV: Black Notebooks 1939–1941.* Trans. R. Rojcewicz. Bloomington: Indiana University Press (2017). GA 96, *Überlegungen XII-XV (Schwarze Hefte 1939–1941)* (2014).

[1940]. *Nietzsche.* Volume IV. Ed. D. F. Krell. San Francisco: Harper & Row (1979–1987). GA 48, *Nietzsche: Der Europäische Nihilismus* (1986).

[1941/42a]. *The Event.* Bloomington: Indiana University Press (2013). GA 71, *Das Ereignis* (2009).

[1941/42b]. *Hölderlin's Hymn "Remembrance"* Bloomington: Indiana University Press (2018). GA 52, *Hölderlins Hymne "Andenken"* (1982).

[1942/43]. *Parmenides*. Bloomington: Indiana University Press (1992). GA 54, *Parmenides* (1982).

[1943a] *Heraclitus*. London: Bloomsbury Academic (2018). GA 55, *Heraklit* (1979).

[1943b] Die Einzigkeit des Dichters. In GA 75, *Zu Hölderlin – Griechenlandreisen* (2000) 35–44.

[1943/44]. Poverty. In *Heidegger, Translation, and the Task of Thinking*. Ed. F. Schalow. Dordrecht: Springer (2011), 3–10. Die Armut. In GA 73.1, *Zum Ereignis-Denken* (2013), 873–81.

[1945]. Evening Conversation: In a Prisoner of War Camp in Russia, between a Younger and an Older Man. In *Country Path Conversations*. Bloomington: Indiana University Press (2010), 132–160. Abendgespräch in einem Kriegsgefangenenlager in Rußland zwischen einem Jüngeren und einem Älteren. In GA 77, *Feldweg Gespräche* (1995), 205–45.

[1945/46]. Hölderlins Dichtung. Ein Geschick. In GA 75, *Zu Hölderlin – Griechenlandreisen* (2000), 349–65.

[1946]. Letter on Humanism. In *Pathmarks*, ed. William McNeill. 239–76. Cambridge: Cambridge University Press (1998). GA 9, *Wegmarken* (1976), 313–64.

[1949]. Insight into What it is: Bremen Lectures 1949. In *Bremen and Freiburg Lectures*. Bloomington: Indiana University Press (2012), 3–73. GA 79, Einblick in das Was ist. Bremer Vorträge 1949. In *Bremer und Freiburger Vorträge* (1994), 3–78.

[1951]. Logos (Heraclitus, Fragment B 50). In *Early Greek Thinking*. New York: Harper (1975), 59–78. Logos (Heraclitus, Fragment 50). In GA 7, *Vorträge und Aufsätze* (2000), 211–34.

[1951/52]. *What Is Called Thinking?* New York: Harper & Row (1968). *Was heisst Denken?* Tübingen: Niemeyer (1997).

[1953]. Science and Reflection. In *The Question Concerning Technology and Other Essays*. New York: Harper & Row (1977), 155–182. Wissenschaft und Besinnung. In GA 7, *Vorträge und Aufsätze*. (2000), 37–66.

[1953/54]. A Dialogue on Language: Between a Japanese and an Inquirer. In *On the Way to Language*. San Francisco: Harper and Row (1971), 1–56. Aus einem Gespräch von der Sprache: Zwischen einem Japaner und einem Fragenden. In *GA 12, Unterwegs zur Sprache* (1985), 79–146.

[1955a]. Gelassenheit. In GA, 16, *Reden und andere Zeugnisse eines Lebensweges 1910–1976* (2000), 517–529. Memorial Address. In *Discourse on Thinking*. New York: Harper & Row (1966), 43–57.

[1955b] *What Is Philosophy?* Lanham: Rowman & Littlefield (2003). Bilingual edition: *Was ist das, die Philosophie?*

[1957]. "A Recollective 'Vita' 1957." In *Becoming Heidegger*. Ed. T. Kisiel & T. Sheehan. Seattle: Noesis Press (2010), 10–11. Vorwort zur ersten Ausgabe der „Frühen Schriften" (1972). In GA 1, *Frühe Schriften* (1978), 55–57. The content of these two texts are the same, but they do not completely correspond to each other.

[1957/58]. Notizen zu Klee / Notes on Klee. Trans. M., Acosta López et. al. *Philosophy Today* 61(1) (2017), 7–17.

1959. *Gelassenheit*. Pfullingen: Verlag Günther Neske.

[1960]. Bild und Wort. In GA 74, *Zum Wesen der Sprache und zur Frage nach der Kunst* (2010), 183–87.

[1962a]. Traditional Language and Technological Language. *Journal of Philosophical Research* 23 (1998), 129–45. *Überlieferte Sprache und Technische Sprache*. St. Gallen: Erker (1989).

[1962b] *Sojourns: The Journey to Greece*. New York: State University of New York Press (2005). Aufenthalte. In GA 75, *Zu Hölderlin – Griechenlandreisen*. *Gesamtausgabe* (2000), 213–46.

[1963]. Aus Gesprächen mit einem Buddhistischen Mönch. In GA 16, *Reden und andere Zeugnisse eines Lebensweges 1910–1976* (2000), 589–93.

[1966]. Only a God can Save Us – Der Spiegel's Interview with Martin Heidegger. *Philosophy Today* 20(4), 267–84. Spiegel Gespräch mit Martin Heidegger. In GA 16, *Reden und andere Zeugnisse eines Lebensweges 1910–1976* (2000), 652–83.

[1968]. Zur Frage nach der Bestimmung der Sache des Denkens. In GA 16, *Reden und andere Zeugnisse eines Lebensweges 1910–1976* (2000), 695.

2001. *Zollikon Seminars*. *Protocolls-Conversations-Letters*. Evanston: Northwestern University Press. GA 89, *Zollikoner Seminare, Protokolle-Gespräche-Briefe* (2000).

2008. *Letters to his Wife 1915–1970*. Cambridge: Polity Press. *Mein liebes Seelchen: Briefe Martin Heideggers an seine Frau Elfride 1915–1970*. Stuttgart: DVA (2005).

2013. GA 73.1, *Zum Ereignis-Denken*.

2015. GA 97, *Anmerkungen I-V.*

2016. Ausgewählte Briefe von Martin und Fritz Heidegger. In *Heidegger und der Antisemitismus*. Ed. W. Homolka. & A. Heidegger. Freiburg: Herder, 11–177.

2020. GA 100, *Vigiliae und Notturno ("Schwarze Hefte" 1952/53 bis 1957)*.

Heidegger, Martin, & Fink, Eugen. 1979. *Heraclitus Seminar 1966/67*. Alabama: University of Alabama Press. *Heraklit*. In GA 15, *Seminare* (1986), 9–266.

Heidegger, Martin, & Löwith, Karl. 2021. *Correspondence 1919–1973*. Lanham: Rowman & Littlefield.

Heller, Peggy. 2010. *The Russian Dawn.* In *The Struggle for the West: A Divided and Contested Legacy.* Ed. C. S. Browning & M. Lehti. London: Routledge, 33–52.

Hesse, Hermann. [1916]. Remembrance of India. In H. Hesse, *Autobiographical Writings.* London: Pan Books (1975), 68–72.

Hoch, Erna M. 1991. *Sources and Resources. A Western Psychiatrist's Search for Meaning in the Ancient Indian Scriptures.* Chur: Rüegger.

Imamichi, Tomonobu. 2004. *In Search of Wisdom: One Philosopher's Journey.* Trans. Mary E. Foster. Tokyo: International House of Japan.

Jaspers, Karl. 1949. *Vom Ursprung und Ziel der Geschichte.* Munich: Piper.

Kitayama, Junyū. 1934. *Metaphysik des Buddhismus. Versuch einer philosophischen Interpretation der Lehre Vasubandhus und seiner Schule.* Stuttgart: W. Kohlhammer.

Keyserling, Hermann. 1919. *Das Reisetagebuch eines Philosophen.* Two volumes. Darmstadt: Reichl.

Kojève, Alexandre. 2018. *The Religious Metaphysics of Vladimir Solovyov.* Trans. I. Merlin & M. Pozdniakov. Cham: Palgrave.

Kraemer, Joel L. 2003. The Islamic Context of Medieval Jewish Philosophy. In *The Cambridge Companion to Medieval Jewish Philosophy.* Ed. D. H. Frank & O. Leaman. Cambridge: Cambridge University Press, 38–68.

Laks, André. 2018. *The Concept of Presocratic Philosophy: Its Origin, Development, and Significance.* Trans. Glenn W. Most. Princeton: Princeton University Press.

Laertius, Diogenes. 1972. *Lives of Eminent Philosophers.* Vol. I. Trans. R. D. Hicks. Cambridge, MA: Harvard University Press.

2021. *Lives of Eminent Philosophers: An Edited Translation.* Ed. & trans. S. A. White. Cambridge: Cambridge University Press.

Love, Jeff (Ed.). 2017. *Heidegger in Russia and Eastern Europe.* Lanham: Rowman & Littlefield.

Ma, Lin. 2008. *Heidegger on East-West Dialogue: Anticipating the Event.* London: Routledge.

2019. Going Under toward the Abyssal Question. *Journal of the British Society for Phenomenology* 50(4), 358–77.

2021. Thinking through Heidegger's "Untergang." *Philosophical Forum* 52, 65–78.

2023. Heidegger on the *Abendland* (West) and the *Abendländische* Philosophy. Paper presented at "Questioning 'Western Philosophy' Conference" held from April 28 to April 30 in Worcester College, Oxford.

Ma, Lin & van Brakel, Jaap. 2014. Out of the *Ge-stell*? The Role of the East in Heidegger's *das andere Denken. Philosophy East and West* 64(3), 527–62.

Marchand, Suzanne L. 2001. German Orientalism and the Decline of the West. *Proceedings of the American Philosophical Society* 145(4), 465–73.

2009. *German Orientalism in the Age of Empire.* Cambridge: Cambridge University Press.

May, Reinhard. 1989. *Ex Oriente Lux: Heideggers Werk unter Ostasiatischem Einfluss.* Wiesbaden: Franz Steiner Verlag.

1996. *Heidegger's Hidden Sources: East Asian Influences on His Work.* London: Routledge.

McGetchin, D. T. Bavaj. 2015. 'Orient' and 'Occident', 'East' and 'West' in the Discourse of German Orientalists, 1790–1930. In *Germany and 'the West': The History of a Modern Concept.* Ed. Riccardo Bavai & Martina Steber. New York: Berghahn, 111–23.

Mehta, Jarava Lal. 1992. *J. L. Mehta on Heidegger, Hermeneutics and Indian tradition.* Ed. W. J. Jackson. Leiden: Brill.

Mirsepassi, Seyed Ali. 2019. *Iran's Troubled Modernity: Debating Ahmad Fardid's Legacy.* Cambridge: Cambridge University Press.

Misch, Georg. 1926. *Der Weg in die Philosophie.* Leipzig: Teubner.

Momigliano, Arnaldo. 1975. *Alien Wisdom. The Limits of Hellenization.* Cambridge: Cambridge University Press.

Moore, Ian Alexander. 2019. Homesickness, Interdisciplinarity, and the Absolute: Heidegger's Relation to Schlegel and Novalis. In *Brill's Companion to German Romantic Philosophy.* Ed. E. Millán. Leiden/Boston: Brill, 280–310.

Moser et. al. Eds. 2019. *Heidegger in the Islamicate World.* London: Rowman & Littlefield.

Nietzsche, Friedrich. [1870]. *The Dionysiac World View.* In *The Birth of Tragedy and Other Writings.* Cambridge: Cambridge University Press (1999), 117–39. *Die Dionysische Weltanschauung.* In *Sämtliche Werke. Kritische Studienausgabe. Band 1: Die Geburt der Tragödie. Unzeitgemäße Betrachtungen I–IV. Nachgelassene Schriften 1870–1873.* Berlin: Walter De Gruyter (1988), 553–77.

[1872]. *The Birth of Tragedy.* In *The Birth of Tragedy and Other Writings.* Cambridge: Cambridge University Press (1999), 1–116. Die Geburt der Tragödie. In *Sämtliche Werke. Kritische Studienausgabe. Band 1.* Berlin: Walter De Gruyter (1988), 9–156.

[1873]. *Philosophy in the Tragic Age of the Greeks.* Washington, DC: Regnery Publishing (1962). Die Philosophie im Tragischen Zeitalter der Griechen. In *Nachgelassene Schriften 1870 – 1873.* Berlin: Walter De Gruyter (1988), 293–366.

1968. *The Will to Power.* Trans. W. Kaufmann & R. J. Hollingdale. New York: Vintage Books.

Okakura, Kakuzō. 1919. *Das Buch vom Tee*. Leipzig: Insel. (Original English version: Okakura, Kakuzō. 1906. *The Book of Tea*. London: Putman's sons.)

Parkes, Graham. Ed. 1987. *Heidegger and Asian Thought*. Honolulu: University of Hawaii Press.

Petzet, Heinrich Wiegand. 1993. *Encounters and Dialogues with Martin Heidegger 1929–1976*. Trans. P. Emad and K. Maly. Chicago: The University of Chicago Press.

Plaenckner, Reinhold von. 1870. *Lao-Tse Tao-Te-King. Der Weg zur Tugend*. Leipzig: F. A. Brockhaus.

Polt, Richard. 2019. *Time and Trauma*. London: Rowman & Littlefield.

Said, Edward W. 1979. *Orientalism*. New York: Vintage Books.

Salamun, K. 2022. *Karl Jaspers: Physician, Psychologist, Philosopher, Political Thinker*. Berlin: Palgrave Macmillan.

Sartre, Jean-Paul. [1948]. *"What is Literature?" and Other Essays*. Cambridge, MA: Harvard University Press (1988).

Schlegel, Frederick von [1808]. *The Aesthetic and Miscellaneous Works of Frederick von Schlegel*. Trans E. J. Millington. Cambridge: Cambridge University Press (2014).

Sdvižkov, Denis. 2015. Russian and German Ideas of the West in the Long Nineteenth Century. In *Germany and 'the West': The History of a Modern Concept*. Ed. Riccardo & Steber, Martina. 97–110. New York: Berghahn Books.

Silk, M. S. & Stern J. P. 2016. *Nietzsche on Tragedy*. Cambridge: Cambridge University Press.

Trawny, Peter. 2017. The Universal and Annihilation: Heidegger's Being-Historical Anti-Semitism. In *Heidegger's Black Notebooks*. Ed. A. J. Mitchell & P. Trawny. New York: Columbia University Press, 1–17.

Ular, Alexander. 1903. *Die Bahn und der rechte Weg*. Leipzig: Insel-Verlag (1912).

Unamuno, Miguel de. [1924]. *Selected Works of Miguel de Unamuno. Volume 5: The Agony of Christianity and Essays on Faith*. Ed. A. Kerrigan & M. Nozick. Princeton: Princeton University Press (1974).

Unruh, Patrick. 2017. *Register zur Martin Heidegger Gesamtausgabe*. Frankfurt: Vittorio Klostermann.

Von Strauss, Victor. [1870]. *Lao-Tse's Tao Te King*. Leipzig: Verlag der "Asia Major" (1924).

Warminski, Andrzej. 1987. *Readings in Interpretation. Hölderlin, Hegel, Heidegger*. Minneapolis: University of Minnesota Press.

West, M. L. 1971. *Early Greek Philosophy and the Orient*. Oxford: Oxford University Press.

Wilhelm, Richard. 1912. *Dschuang Dsi: Das wahre Buch vom südlichen Blütenland*. Jena: Verlegt bei Eugen Diederichs.

Williams, Robert C. 1997. *Russia Imagined: Art, Culture, and National Identity, 1840–1995*. New York: Peter Lang.

Wrathall, Mark A. Ed. 2021. *The Cambridge Heidegger Lexicon*. Cambridge: Cambridge University Press.

Xia, Kejun. 2021. Heideggers Ungebrauch: Daoistisches Denken im Angesicht der Schwarzen Hefte. *Deutsche Zeitschrift Für Philosophie* 69(5), 801–17.

Acknowledgements

I am grateful to Daniel O. Dahlstrom and Filippo Casati for their invitation to contribute to the Series of *Elements in the Philosophy of Martin Heidegger*. I wish to thank two anonymous reviewers for their constructive suggestions on an early draft. At a later stage, D. Dahlstrom read the whole text and I have benefited considerately from his feedback. I appreciate in particular D. Dahlstrom's – as a leading Heidegger specialist – openness to my East-West perspective on Heidegger's thinking. I am also indebted to Jaap van Brakel for crosschecking some of my readings of Heidegger's German texts and for his sustained encouragement for my academic pursuit. Last but not least, I thank my faculty – the School of Philosophy of Renmin University of China – for granting me research time to work on this Element.

Cambridge Elements ☰

The Philosophy of Martin Heidegger

About the editors

Filippo Casati

Lehigh University

Filippo Casati is an Assistant Professor at Lehigh University. He has published an array of articles in such venues as The British Journal for the History of Philosophy, Synthese, Logic et Analyse, Philosophia, Philosophy Compass and The European Journal of Philosophy. He is the author of Heidegger and the Contradiction of Being (Routledge) and, with Daniel O. Dahlstrom, he edited Heidegger on logic (Cambridge University Press).

Daniel O. Dahlstrom

Boston University

Daniel O. Dahlstrom, John R. Silber Professor of Philosophy at Boston University, has edited twenty volumes, translated Mendelssohn, Schiller, Hegel, Husserl, Heidegger, and Landmann-Kalischer, and authored Heidegger's Concept of Truth (2001), The Heidegger Dictionary (2013; second extensively expanded edition, 2023), Identity, Authenticity, and Humility (2017) and over 185 essays, principally on 18th-20th century German philosophy. With Filippo Casati, he edited Heidegger on Logic (Cambridge University Press).

About the series

A continual source of inspiration and controversy, the work of Martin Heidegger challenges thinkers across traditions and has opened up previously unexplored dimensions of Western thinking. The Elements in this series critically examine the continuing impact and promise of a thinker who transformed early twentieth-century phenomenology, spawned existentialism, gave new life to hermeneutics, celebrated the truthfulness of art and poetry, uncovered the hidden meaning of language and being, warned of "forgetting" being, and exposed the ominously deep roots of the essence of modern technology in Western metaphysics. Concise and structured overviews of Heidegger's philosophy offer original and clarifying approaches to the major themes of Heidegger's work, with fresh and provocative perspectives on its significance for contemporary thinking and existence.

Printed in the United States
by Baker & Taylor Publisher Services